Maxime Rovere is a philosopher who has dedicated his life to studying the ways we interact, through both the history of philosophy (Spinoza and others in the Early Enlightenment) as well as in contemporary ethics, and now in turning his attention to the scourge of all ages: idiots. Associate Researcher at the École Normale Supérieure (Lyon), he was Council of Humanities Visiting Fellow at Princeton University in 2019 and a fellow at the Netherlands Institute for Advanced Studies in 2021.

David Bellos is a translator and biographer, and is Meredith Howland Pyne Professor of French Literature and Professor of Comparative Literature at Princeton University. His book, *Is That a Fish in Your Ear?* is a brilliant account of the way translation is at the heart of everything we do.

How
to
Deal
With
Idiots

(AND STOP BEING ONE YOURSELF)

Maxime Rovere
Translated by **David Bellos**

PROFILE BOOKS

This paperback edition first published in 2023

First published in Great Britain in 2021 by
Profile Books Ltd
29 Cloth Fair
London
EC1A 7JQ
www.profilebooks.co.uk

First published in France as *Que faire des cons: Pour ne pas en
rester un soi-même*
© Flammarion, Paris, 2019

English language translation copyright © David Bellos, 2021

1 3 5 7 9 10 8 6 4 2

CPI Group (UK) Ltd, Croydon, CR0 4YY

The moral right of the author has been asserted.

A CIP catalogue record for this book is available from the
British Library.

ISBN 978 1 78816 714 7
eISBN 978 1 78283 808 1

Translator's Note

Maxime Rovere's profound and entertaining essay tackles a broad problem for which the French language possesses a single term. It's a word often said aloud in anger, disgust or amusement, and you can write and print it in many contexts – but you'll not hear it uttered in news broadcasts, or see it printed in the regular press. Using this vigorous and still not quite proper word as the title and topic of a philosophical essay is almost scandalous, and also sets a problem for translation. To call someone *con* in French may indicate that their intellectual faculties fall short of the full hamper, or else that their behaviour fails to come up to the mark. Because the French word has both these meanings, it creates a deep connection between them – and that is what this book is really about. English, on the other hand, has a superabundance of terms for the uncountable manifestations of stupidity and boorishness in our fellow humans, without offering one overarching term for the fundamental problem that Maxime Rovere dissects in this book. My solution has been to multiply the object of discussion, usually by two, so as to speak not of *cons*, but of jerks *and* idiots, oafs *and* boneheads, louts *and* fuckwits, and so forth. Nonetheless, the singular focus of this treatise is on how to face up to the always united front of stupidity and incivility in interpersonal relationships and social life.

David Bellos

Princeton, December 2020

INTRODUCTION

Philosophers have never taken the issue I tackle in this book very seriously because they are mainly concerned, as they should be, with the positive powers of the mind. That said, philosophers' endeavours to understand and explore the different ways that 'understanding' can be understood have not left idiocy entirely out of the equation. This is for the good reason that even in the woolliest approach to the problem, understanding and stupidity are by definition in inverse proportion to one another: understanding increases in lockstep with a reduction in idiocy. However, that is also why philosophers have almost always given their adversary an entirely negative definition, one that presupposes that you share the philosopher's starting position: that of a person who is *theoretically* intelligent. Without giving an extended history of the philosophy of idiots, we can still say that philosophers have variously presented stupidity as an obstacle to knowledge, to moral progress, to healthy discussion and to life in society, identifying it by such terms as *public opinion, prejudice, pride, superstition, intolerance, the passions, dogmatism, pedantry, nihilism*, and so on. In doing so they have of course thrown light on many aspects of stupidity. But because they have always intellectualised the issue (which is quite natural for masters of thought), they have not been able to see it in the light that reveals it to be a genuine problem.

To put it simply, the problem is not stupidity: the problem is stupid people. And this of course presents its own challenges. Because whatever definition of stupidity you start from, you end up with the same conclusion: stupidity must be battled and beaten down by every possible and imaginable means and by all the human and non-human powers that can be brought to bear on it. The Latin saying *stultitia delenda est* expresses a fierce and limitless hatred, telling us that *stupidity must be destroyed*. But what then about stupid people? Real living idiots – that's to say, the ones we stumble over in daily life or encounter on trains and planes, the jerks who sit at other desks in our offices and the blockheads with whom we share our lives and who may be found, alas, in our own families and yes, even among those we choose as friends and lovers ... You see who I mean? Who would say they must be *annihilated*? Anyone who did so would be not only an unrivalled idiot but a criminal as well.

Idiots thus constitute a far more tricky and far more significant problem from a philosophical point of view than stupidity as such. Their existence as plain stupid and often aggressive individuals is an extremely complex theoretical problem because it is circular in shape. In fact, whenever you encounter a jerk or an idiot, a switch occurs that immediately undercuts your intelligence (I use the word in its widest sense, to mean *a disposition to understand*). Obviously, I do not wish to go so far as to insult you, dear reader, but you have to admit that from the moment you identify another person as an idiot, you are no longer *engaged* with that person, but in a *situation* where your own attempt to understand is grievously impaired. This is because one of the main characteristics of boneheadedness – and it is important to use everyday language to name it – is that it sucks up your own analytic capabilities and, by some strange quirk, obliges you to talk in its own language, to play along with it. In a word, idiocy is a trap. Getting out of it is terribly difficult. I face the problem in my own home. I share a flat with a numbskull (not for much longer, thank goodness). And so I have decided to set aside my more abstruse scholarly activities in order to do you (and me) the favour of explaining why the problem is so hard – perhaps the hardest problem of all. I do so in the hope of finding a way out of it.

However, before getting down to the specific problems that jerks set us – and which I truly believe to be as serious as the weightiest topics that philosophers have ever tackled – I must first alert you to the fact that in this book I am dealing with stupidity in the real world, not in an ideal world. In other words, I am fully aware that insofar as it is a moral, political and social issue, stupidity must be thwarted. We must establish ways of organising life in society that discourage young people from becoming blockheads – especially since, irrespective of their social backgrounds, they may well be the offspring of assholes and fools themselves. I acknowledge that this is a pressing matter indeed. On the other hand, we must not allow the efforts to foster intelligence on a broad front to obscure the limitations of this project. The implementation and effectiveness of anti-idiot measures are hostage to many factors: but there will never be a society in which one part of the population – even if it has only a single member – is not viewed by some other part of the population – again, even if it consists of just a single individual – as irremediably thick. In that sense, despite stupidity being theoretically solvable and despite the appropriateness and legitimacy of the efforts made to stamp it out by thoughtful and well-intentioned people, in the real world it will always be with us.

So we have to grant from the outset that even in the best of all possible worlds and with the best will that can be mustered, you will *always* and *necessarily* bump into nitwits. That is not just because progress never achieves total victory or because idiocy adapts easily to new circumstances. The distinctive feature of stupidity is a specific form of resistance, a blind opposition to anything being done to remedy a situation, including the situation of idiots themselves. So on all occasions, idiots will mount energetic opposition to your efforts, they will try to drown your arguments in endless and specious reasoning, they will try to stifle your benevolence with threats, your kindness with violence, and the common interest with blinkers that undermine the very basis of their own individual interests. In that respect, stupidity is not just a kind of incomprehensible leftover of human evolution; on the contrary, it is one of the main engines of History, a force which despite or rather because of its blindness has won many of the major battles of the past and will surely win many more in times to come. Allow me to sum up the insurmountable permanence of that force by simply saying that *idiots always hunker down.*

Rather inconveniently, this particular feature of stupid people rules out the simpler solutions. Given the way idiots dig in their heels, there is no point pleading for tolerance among the intolerant, or proposing intellectual enlightenment among the superstitious, or preaching open-mindedness to the prejudiced, and so on. Uttering grand declarations or displaying fine feelings serves only to soothe the speaker, and the pleasure that such speechifying provides is just one more opportunity for stupidity to suck in its opponents, trap them in its web and obstruct yet again all attempts to arrive at understanding.

For all these reasons, reconciliation with jerks and idiots is structurally impossible. And as they themselves do not want reconciliation, we will just have to learn to cope with them. But how can we do that? Having made the dolorous admission that idiots exist as a matter of fact, indeed, that they exist necessarily, have always existed and always will, how can we then find the means (it is always already too late to adopt preventive measures) – how can we find the means to cope with fools, boors, blockheads and the like?

If I'd known the answer when I asked the question, I would be one of them. But I do have a few cards up my sleeve all the same: a sketch of a plan, some methods and tools, and familiarity with abstract thought. So let us work together for a while to see if philosophy can come up with clear solutions to this urgent problem.

THREE CONCLUSIONS BEFORE WE EVEN START

'Oi, you, stop shoving!'

'Move down the carriage then!'

'Move? In that crush?'

'Well, *you* stop shoving then!'

'Then *you* move!'

'Then don't shove!'

'Gimme a break!'

'Can't you just move down a bit?'

'But I told you already …'

Stupidity is in the eye of the beholder; stupidity can appear in an infinite number of guises; the biggest idiot of all is the one in the mirror. Now that's been said, we can start to think.

When you picked up this book, you had in mind your own experience of fools and boors. A face and a name may have come to mind ... Your painful experience, which may have involved matters as serious as injustice or suffering, makes you want to get your own back on idiots, which means learning more about them, having a bit of a laugh at their expense, and feeling more intelligent than they are. I share your hope. But before I begin, allow me to draw your attention to a problem inside our problem, namely, a question of definition.

Although it is possible to define stupidity in abstract terms, it is very difficult to say exactly what it is that makes an idiot an idiot. Two things are plain. First, it's obvious that the term 'idiot' is relative to such a degree that there is always someone out there for whom *you* are the idiot – and that is surely why there is no serious study of the topic so far. Secondly, and reciprocally, it's just as clear that we all have our own idiot – by which I mean that we all have a sense of a Being whose outlines may be as fuzzy as that of a ghost but whose existence is far more obvious to us than that of God. Like me, you too would like philosophy to provide a better grasp of a *thing* that appears in our lives in the shape of specific idiots and jerks.

But here is something to puzzle over: from the perspective of a pure intelligence, idiots do not exist. The conceptual form of God sees no stupid people when he looks down upon the world. His infinite understanding instantly grasps the machinery of causes, the connections of factors and the dynamics of interactions that make humans act. With unending benevolence, He who is infinitely wise extends his loving acceptance to all rash inventions, rude gestures, silly remarks, low cunning, and so on. In his omnipotence, he knows that everything has its place in the world, and his confidence in the way the universe works allows him to remember this, even when contemplating ridiculous opinions and absurd human flaws. Idiots don't slip under the radar of the Absolute: they just evaporate under its Perfect Gaze.

But we are no God. It seems obvious that the problem we have with stupid people is that meeting them forces us to appreciate our own limitations. Idiots stand on that bourn beyond which we cannot extend our love or understanding. That leaves us with two alternatives. We could wallow in our own imperfection and be as pathetic as brainless twits who enjoy sniggering at the things they don't understand. Or we could acknowledge the specific force of stupidity, which is to be found in the effect that it has on us as individuals, and resort instead to the opposing force of ideas to trample over stupid people, which is to say, we could try to be not only better than they are but also better than we actually are ourselves.

The second path has a grave drawback: being better is not always entertaining, and on occasions it is frankly a bore. But fear not – I reckon it won't take more than a few relatively jargon-free pages for us to study the existence of idiots as a complex phenomenon.

Even before I begin, however, another problem looms. The sheer variety of forms that stupidity takes surely makes it impossible to study all idiots in one sweep. There are idiots who are so sure they are right that they will not countenance a moment's self-doubt; then there are those who are sure of nothing and query even the simplest truth; then there's a third lot who don't give a damn for the other two groups, or for anything else, even for perfectly avoidable disasters. How can I possibly put all idiots in one basket?

One imaginable solution would be to establish the types and species of stupid people and to group them into families, maybe even to draw a family tree. But in my view, such a typology would have the serious disadvantage of giving to fools and knaves the kind of consistency that they do not possess. If I were to list various different kinds of idiot along with a description of the distinguishing features of each, we would very probably agree about some of them, and jointly identify certain idiot-types or essences (as when sampling perfumes). Unfortunately, that would produce a result directly contrary to our aim: you would be inclined to over-project your own experience, that is to say, you would let yourself believe that you have had to cope with *entities*, not with situations. In other words, the more such a list allows you to recognise the jerks and twits in your own life, the more likely you are to believe that idiots exist in the same way that ostriches and copper beeches exist (which is not the case, as I will show you very soon). Such a belief would result in your moving further away from the perspective of pure intelligence and benevolence, so that the ultimate effect of this book, as of so many others, would be to have you wallow ever deeper in your own prejudices, instead of leading you (and me) towards a little more wisdom.

So classifying idiots won't help us understand them any better, nor will it help us manage the ways in which they intervene in our lives. It's true that in many films, comedy acts and novels there is a typecast fool, a character whose total lack of imagination is designed to prompt others – as if by magic – to creative exploits. But that fact only supports my argument. Philosophy works with *concepts*, not with *characters*. So as to be fair to different cases, I'm planning brief interludes where I can make visible the kinds of experiences I have in mind while working with abstractions. But my aim is not to invent anything. My aim is to understand.

In other words, and despite this being rather unusual in philosophical discourse, I am asking you not to try to define idiots too precisely. Let's leave them to twinkle on in the night sky where each of us can pick out our own star idiots. Let me go even further. To be completely sincere, I don't really give a damn about what idiots are, where they come from, or what unpleasant methods they use to reproduce. All I want is for them to let me live in peace. And yet it is here, precisely, in a tender heart that yearns only to love, that there is a snag, a problem as sharp and nasty as a rusty nail: idiots do not leave us in peace, and they afflict in particular those who would most like to live far away from them. And so, the second axiom of my book is: *idiots are all around and all over us.*

That is indeed a great mystery. How does stupidity make its way in the world, how does it slither and slide and insert its insidious self inside a *theoretically intelligent subject*? To answer this question, we have to start from the point where intelligence stops. And that, dear reader, is why I have already given you three observations that a smarter but less sincere author would have held back until the conclusion. Namely: every one of us is an idiot in someone else's eyes; stupidity has an infinite number of forms; and the main idiot is the one we harbour inside ourselves. These three points are all perfectly correct, but as far as I am concerned, they are of no use at all. What I want from philosophy are precise conceptual techniques that allow me to overcome the weakness in my understanding and the shortfall in benevolence that I experience every time I go past a particular door in my own home and find myself face to face with human idiocy.

HOW IDIOTS TIE US IN KNOTS

There are foolish men who don't want to get into trouble with their wives, and stupid women who try to avoid trouble with their mates; idiots who prefer not to get in a tangle with their kids, and thickos who feel the same about their parents – or their neighbours or their colleagues or their students or their teachers or their bosses or the media or their customers or the police … and because of the desperate efforts they all make to avoid each other, as they retreat, so as to avoid getting into trouble, jerks and idiots bump blindly into each other all the time.

In which it is shown that stupidity is a device used by idiots in order to entrap you. And how to direct your mind so as to begin to find the way out.

I diots crop up without warning, just when you were least expecting them. You weren't ready. You just wanted to get on with whatever you were doing, taking a trip, looking at the scenery, doing your work or enjoying your life – let's say, you just wanted to carry on in your own sweet way. But human idiocy reared its head. Now it doesn't matter whether you were in a good mood or not. Idiocy has riled you up and got you down. If I may be a little more dramatic and precise, it has offended you. Even if your pride makes you want to rise above it all, stupidity always offends you. And the very fact that you are offended by it upsets you; this only increases the offence and makes it worse.

Let's not be squeamish. Let's look at the wound close up. In thousands of instances that arise in the world – a driver cutting in on your lane, a walker giving his dog a kick, or a passer-by dropping litter on the pavement – jerks are people who lack respect for others, who disregard even a common-sense rule, who basically undermine the conditions of life in society. Of course, it has to be said that many of these behaviours are symptoms of deeper problems that don't just depend on the people concerned: difficult and unstable working conditions, leisure and consumption industries unleashed to anxiety-inducing excess, the dismantling of frameworks that regulate person-to-person relations ... To grasp the situation in its entirety, we have to take into account a process whereby not only do idiots destroy the conditions of life in society, but also through which a sick society produces idiots. But the fact that human phenomena arise from specific conditions in no way precludes the real existence of idiots and jerks.

So we have an initial consideration of some importance. A behaviour that we judge to be insufficient marks jerks and idiots as individuals that we can identify, if only fleetingly, as occupying a lower rung on the scale of morality by which we aspire to become fully accomplished human beings (without presupposing that we are anywhere near the top of the scale ourselves).

Before we pursue this any further, we must first quickly answer an objection. Since each of us is always a jerk or an idiot in the eyes of someone (see above), do we really have the right to call anyone else an idiot? In all probability, that blockhead thinks *we* are the idiot. And anyway, who would dare to try to define a 'fully accomplished human being'? If we followed this line of argument to its end, stupidity would exist only in relative terms, and would be entirely dependent on any one person's point of view: it would be a reflection of personal preferences that are valid for a given individual but not for anybody else. But I can live with that! Relativism of this kind does not scare me. I willingly grant you that each of us is someone else's jerk; and yet that does not mean that all idiots are the same. Quite the opposite, in fact: if everybody has his or her own evaluation of idiocy, when such evaluations are compared and contrasted it will necessarily result in a range of agreements and disagreements. So in the sort of urgent, local situation that we are trying to analyse, the idiot is the person who is identified as such by the greatest number of others (allowing for variations). That means that objective stupidity is not something existing in absolute terms and which precedes subjective evaluations, but is produced by the combination of these evaluations, such that you can say that objectivity is located at the intersection of all subjectivities and is what they have in common with each other. So the fact that stupidity is relative does not prevent it having a truth value; on the contrary, it expresses precisely the truth of those relativities. So I conclude once again that we can maintain that idiots really exist, they are people who, even if only in local and fleeting circumstances, are *less* successful than the rest of us in our joint effort to become human. And I reckon that we can all agree that this is so, although each of us may have a different take on the details.

However, there is a curious anomaly in all this. In the situation we have just described, people who think of themselves as witnesses of stupidity, as it were, should be in a position of superiority. For if a person is identified (if only for an instant) as being by virtue of some behaviour on a lower rung of the moral scale that measures our striving towards perfection as human beings, then that should signify that others are on some higher rung. So when an individual behaves in an abusive, counter-productive or dangerous way, we should put our superior status to some use, and take action to remedy the situation and, without recourse to anger, prevent the jerk or the idiot from doing harm. But that is not what happens. Why not? Because weakness and moral inferiority do not say everything about idiocy. We must note a second, important determinant: idiocy is not just weakness, it is also ugliness. It can be defined as the repulsive face of human weakness.

That is where the knottiness of the real problem is to be found. Astounded all of a sudden by judging someone as an inferior being (with *greater or lesser* reason, but never without *any* reason), we are just as flummoxed by the awareness that we are experiencing a kind of withdrawal, scorn or disgust. This catches us out. We know and we feel that we are better than the swine who doesn't flush the toilet, better than the grand lady who thinks she can get away with anything because she has money; and yet our own worthiness does not allow us to overcome or vanquish idiocy. No sir! It's the other way round! The more they exasperate us and the more we yearn to stop them in their tracks or to wipe them off the face of the earth, the more we identify them as jerks and idiots: as beings who cause the waters of our benevolence and love to ebb as fast as the tide at Southend. Boorishness and stupidity may be grounded on formal moral judgements, but they provoke at the very same instant an affective relation – in other words, an emotion – that is by definition negative, an instinctive feeling, a burst of impatience that makes us hunger to renounce our common humanity. It may be a healthy reaction or it may be suicidal, but in the instant we don't really care to know which it is. No matter what you do, you simply can't stand jerks and idiots: *stultitia delenda est.*

That's when a strange mechanism springs into action. I'm going to describe it several times over using different images so as to avoid various pitfalls. Let's go back to where we were, gathered around the twit or boor who poisoned our lives, and in agreement that we should rank him or her on a lower rung than the one we cling to ... But at the very moment an idiot appears repugnant to us, we in our turn start to lose a capacity for empathy. It's true! The more you realise that the idiot is an idiot and the jerk a jerk, the more you depart from your own human ideal, and the more you become – in lockstep – a hostile being, that's to say, a jerk or an idiot (the proof of it being that you turn into the idiot's idiot). That blot on the landscape does nothing but offend you and makes you want to eliminate it from your field of vision, if only to feel less uncomfortable. That idiot is getting on your nerves, making you sick – but the more you withdraw, the more he insults you. So you retreat further, wading ever deeper into the quagmire of your own contempt. How can you not detest the other person, since it is entirely their fault? And the more you hate, the deeper you sink.

These quicksands exemplify a process that tells us, as a conclusion to this first chapter, why it is so difficult to make any progress when faced with idiots and assholes. In fact, the impressions we receive from the sight of human imperfection instantly constitute a posture that lowers and diminishes not only the being we observe as an object, from the outside, but also the observing subject, the supposed spectator of human stupidity. What that means is that it is structurally impossible simply to *witness* an instance of doltish or brainless behaviour. It is a contradiction in terms, in effect, to be a neutral observer of stupidity. The value judgement that allows you to identify someone as a boor or a thickhead has already predisposed you *against* them. Moreover, this absence of neutrality does not leave you untainted – far from it. Your judgement itself is an instant signal of the lessening of the love and benevolence you are capable of displaying, in the here and now, towards the dickhead in front of you. So the reason why idiots are such a calamity is that they constitute a dynamic problem which, at the very moment it arises as a problem, destroys the conditions necessary for its solution. From which I deduce the first of the sentences that I shall call *take-aways* because they have been specially shaped for youngsters to go paint them on walls when in urgent need – and which you can also pin to the inside of your eyelids so as to never forget them:

---

1 **Do not try to educate idiots**
Change the situation, not the person

HOW TO RECOVER FROM STUPEFACTION

'Excuse me, hi ... Wonderful beach, isn't it?'

'Yeah.'

'It's incredible, all that space ... it's so huge ...'

'...'

'I can see why you've brought your stereo. It's nice to listen to music.'

'Yeah.'

'Yes, I like music too. I brought my headphones.
But ... um ... is the shadow of our parasol not going to bother you?'

'Nah. Anyway, shadows move.'

'But could you ... well, maybe it would be more comfortable for everyone ... if you could ...'

'If we what?'

In which will be shown the unconscious reasoning that makes you confuse suffering and evil; and why idiots are events like any others.

The circular problem I've called a quicksand comes from the fact that there is no charge sheet for idiocy: because of its highly contagious nature, idiots transmit idiocy almost immediately. Just identifying a person as an idiot sets you on track to become one soon after, since the identification causes you to lose your cool and your analytic abilities. So as you struggle to get free of assholes, you foster the emergence of yet another – the one inside you. It's a nightmare that's scarier than science fiction, but it explains and elucidates your panic reaction.

The effort to break the vicious circle has given rise to a number of observations in the realms of philosophy, religion, myth, literature, art and elsewhere. To sum them up very briefly: no human being has ever failed to notice that we tend to like people who are likeable and to smile at people who smile. Once again, we are caught in a circle – a virtuous one, on this occasion – where the phenomenon we call love (or benevolence, if you prefer) is capable of self-perpetuation solely from the interaction of its elements. But since jerks and idiots set off the opposite phenomenon and drag us into hostility by self-perpetuating responses, the solution must necessarily lie in a reversal of the affective dynamics.

The way out of the problem should then simply be a switch into reverse, as recommended in various places – to respond to hate with love, to forgive those that sin against us, to look at things from the other side, turn the other cheek, or, in brief, to smile at the obnoxious wretch who's getting on your nerves. Only your own generosity can help you – not just the culprit, but you too – to recover a higher standard of humanity.

Unfortunately, this proposal, which I hereby dub *switching*, entails a difficulty which we all know only too well. Moral switching presupposes thwarting all the forces that tend towards conflict so as to break the chain of cause and effect; in other words, to overturn the natural order of things and put them into reverse. Now that seems very hard to do, and it is, in addition, logically absurd. Where, I ask you, will you find enough strength just to give a sympathetic wink to the jerk who despises you, or to smile at the thickhead who's knowingly made a pig's breakfast of your application form? Where is the reservoir of the strength you would need to face down a fucking idiot, seeing that we have defined idiocy by its capacity for expansion, that is to say, by the way it *saps* the moral energy of its adversary? The truth is that invoking moral switching presupposes what it is supposed to engender: it grants you the strength to do what you should do *in theory* – while granting simultaneously that you do not possess it *in fact*.

That's why in every tradition or culture where it arises, moral switching pertains to the logic of sainthood and grace. It implies a strength that is beyond you, that is not entirely you and maybe not entirely human, which takes over just when you are found wanting. That being so, in order to accomplish moral switching, you have to channel a power that is more than mine, more than yours, and maybe more than human. Call it God, or the gods, or the spirits, or the Direction of History or whatever moral virtue, artistic inspiration or rational power you like. The additional energy that allows you to perform a moral switch has to come from somewhere, and that somewhere can only be *elsewhere* (that's to say, not in you, not in me, and not remotely in idiots).

Many great-hearted men and women have written about this and I do not wish to linger on it. All I need do is draw your attention to what is for me the main point, specifically, the interesting, not to say brilliant, proposal contained within the idea of moral switching. For the latter does not just express a pious wish. It allows the mechanism of idiocy to be seen in a light that does not require forces to be thwarted for them to be inverted. Here's how.

As I said, stupid behaviour does an injury that weakens us morally. However, despite our first impression, that does not mean that it robs us of our strength *absolutely*. To be sure, idiocy by definition is a hurt, and idiots most often hurt each other. But that does not mean that stupidity is *absolutely* evil: we should beware of letting things run away with us. For there is a great difference between *causing injury* and *being evil*. Up to now, in the panic we've been in, we've failed to make that distinction. Fools and knaves do things badly (that is the value judgement our intelligence allows us to produce) and by the same token they do bad to us (that is the affective determination, describing the relationship that holds between idiots and ourselves). But we cannot deduce from these two evident truths that jerks and nitwits embody a determination of absolute, universal evil. Nonetheless, that's what you think … Go on, admit it! That is because evil as an abstract notion is a determination that pays no heed to relationships: it is by definition valid without reference to its context of emergence. Leaving aside the question of the solidity of the notion itself, you have to admit that your specific pain (arising from the fact that your ex is pestering you about the old vacuum cleaner, or that your colleague makes you repeat the same instructions over and over without ever doing what you tell him) has caused you to make a mental transition from a relational framework (the idiot's specific action and your specific reaction to his or her existence) to an unconditional declaration: *stultitia delenda est*, universal stupidity must be destroyed absolutely, and in addition and if at all possible, this particular jerk must be wiped off the face of the earth. This kind of mental slip or slide is what is called an induction, because it goes from the particular to the general. But this induction is false. By means of this unconscious logical operation, the germ or virus of idiocy has infected you too. You are claiming universal validity for a truth that is only relative, and you are placing yourself (admittedly, without realising it) in the position of a Judge of the Universe. Well, taking your own opinion to be an absolute is one of the subjective definitions of the asshole, as it corresponds precisely to the self-image of such lamentable individuals.

Aha! You must now be ready to grant that despite your pain, you cannot absolutely deduce from it that the existence of an idiot is a manifestation of evil, or even that the idiocy exhibited by an imbecile is an evil ('idiocy' here refers to the mental condition, not to any crimes committed in its name). This point has one great merit, for it allows us to freeze or stabilise a situation that I described earlier as one of shifting sands. We have just discovered that it is caused less by interpersonal interaction than by the stupefaction that hits you the moment you are hurt (shocked, affronted) by some person's behaviour and which puts your mind in a whirl by directing your attention to that hurt. In fact, the vicious circle that arises between you and the idiot is fostered and fed by another conflict within you, one that saps your energy as it drains away your good will. Because you felt bad, you reckoned the existence of the idiot was bad too, or if you prefer, that it was a mishap. That's why I gave this chapter the heading 'stupefaction'. The quicksand is an illusion created by panic that feeds on itself. Because you didn't know how to escape from it, you reckoned you could not extricate yourself without destroying either the idiot or the idiocy. This train of thought is natural and necessary, but it has led your thinking into a dead end, because it is simply wrong.

The irreducible negativity of stupidity is rather an event which, like any other event, is not an evil *in itself*, although it is a pain. As we all know, any event is ambivalent: it can turn out for good or for ill; more or less well, or more or less badly; the outcome of an event is never pre-set, even though it is entwined in chains of causes and effects; in sum, an event is pure reality insofar as it emerges unwrapped, pliant, and susceptible to change. And when it takes the form of a loudmouth getting you down by telling tasteless jokes all day long, well, that idiot is obviously susceptible to change, he's basically inviting it. Yes, he is summoning you – not to violence (that would shove you into the quicksand) nor to sainthood (mind you, if you've got it in you, don't hold back) – but to a *test*. You should see your jerk as an opportunity to test the moral values to which you quite properly refer when you call the jerk a jerk and which in your striving to become human you seek to attribute to yourself. Whence I deduce:

> *2* **When idiots stand in your way**
> **Moral worth comes into play**

WHY MISFORTUNE CAN BE GOOD FOR YOU

There are some idiots who unload their accumulated frustrations on others, who submerge the whole world in a tide of resentment and drown you in a flood of backbiting, mesmerised as they are by the sheer quantity, the truly infinite amount of slander they can heap on other people, and who also end up finding you a delightful fellow, simply because you didn't get a word in edgeways. Later on, when their bile has built up anew, they'll go find some other listener and they'll pour out a flood of backbiting and the truly infinite amount of slander they can heap on other people and they'll also say how and why you were such a disappointment to them.

In which it is revealed that stupidity cannot be observed,
it can only have accomplices. And that is why we are not
indifferent to it, and wish to act.

If you have read this far and understood at least a little of what has been said, you will not disagree with the idea that jerks are inferior beings, but they are not a sufficient reason for giving up hope for the whole universe. Once the panic has ebbed, you grasp, first, that idiots create a moral differentiation (for jerks *are* inferior); second, that they challenge you (to ward off the effects of the difference); and third, that their stupidity itself gives you an advantage and puts you in the lead. If you have understood this much, you have regained control over your future. And if you are not already feeling in a position of strength, please reread what I just wrote.

With all due respect to mystical advocates of grace and proponents of moral will, you now no longer have to find more strength than you possess. You have learned to distinguish between relative and absolute evil, and you understand that the more an idiot is idiotic, the more he or she requires a response in the here and now, from you and from nobody else, that is designed to prevent them from doing more harm. It doesn't matter from here on that the jerks are an insult to humanity. We now see that they are *absolutely* the specific idiots who currently challenge your own humanity. The humanity that you wish to bring to full completeness in yourself.

The notion of challenge thus helps us revise entirely our original description and to extricate ourselves from shifting sands once and for all without recourse to a moral switch. It's not just a matter of relativising idiocy. The issue is to distract your attention from the negative part of the interaction (to wit, the stupidity of the jerk in question) which, by surprising you, turns poisonous and sets off a circular process of rejection which turns you into an idiot as well. Without doing anything else at the start, you have only to refocus your mind on what matters, namely the challenge that any such event throws at your humanity. I talk of a *challenge* so as to highlight the personal and even intimate dimension that an encounter with another creates. It is not simply a random opportunity for you to take action. We're dealing with a person – even if it is someone you've never seen before and will never see again – who is engaged in an interaction with you, and with nobody else.

You know now that the first thing to have in mind when you encounter a boor or a fool is to remember that your opponent is sinking into a quagmire (which one? who cares?) and that in these circumstances you are in a sense the only hope there is in our joint aspiration towards the human. So as not to put your own foot in the bog, you must therefore take cognisance of the fact that an idiot is evidence of a malfunction, an anomaly, in what you conceive of as humanity. And who must defend this conception of the human, if not you? That's why it is for you, and for you alone, to rebuild peace and harmony. Of course it is! You can't expect an oaf or a twit to do it for you, since they are, respectively, a twit and an oaf. As a result, the lower they have sunk and the greater their stupidity, the more you need to be wise, that is to say, you need to understand things, so as to move them on to another place.

Whereas moral switching presupposes an excess of love that can only be supplied by general principles (love of God, universal harmony, reason, pragmatism, strength, and so on), the idea of a challenge incites you on the contrary to particularise your approach to the phenomenon so far as to take it as *exclusively* addressed to you – as if the hooligan at issue was a certified letter that you alone were entitled to receive. Some might say it was sent by God, others would say it was Fate. For my part, I assure you that stupidity has no witnesses, and that amounts to the same thing. It means that when a thickhead arises, you cannot observe him or her from the outside; you are not the *so-called observer* that you think you are. You'll say you have no role at all in the idiocy of the other; and I'll reply, oh yes, you do, because you're the one who is aware of it. In that sense, even if this is an utterly repugnant thought, the jerk is one half of the game – and you are the other.

Of course you deny what I just said. But in order to do so, you have to make a dangerously erroneous induction by discounting the specific qualities of the situation you are in when confronted by a nincompoop. So, to complete the formula by means of which I wish to wake you from your self-hypnosis and bring you back to your senses, let me tell you the really shocking news: *stupidity has no witnesses because it has only accomplices.* I know from personal experience how offensive this news is. But we must ourselves extract from the living flesh the thorn that causes us such pain. The time has therefore come for me to turn your attention to your own role in the situation.

What makes you furious (and also makes your fury useless) is a particular idea of responsibility, through which you wish to exempt and discharge yourself from the idiocy of the fuckwit you are up against. You reckon it's not for you to settle the conflict, because you're not the one who started it. You imagine that if you were to take the first step towards pacification, you would be giving credence to the lurking suspicion that you are also a bit at fault for the other's stupidity, that really it's *all* your fault, since you're the one who had to take the peace-making initiative.

You know what? Your resistance is justified. I agree with you entirely. An idiot is morally responsible for being an idiot. Anyway, idiots are always the instigators of conflict. Of course the idiocy is all theirs, four-square. But you would be wrong to imagine that this is of the slightest importance. Once an idiot has entered your life, the time for lamentation is past. The fault may well be his or hers, if you really insist on knowing, but the life in question is *yours.* So train your mind ONLY on the situation as it concerns you, and use it to work out your margin for manoeuvre and to pick the strategy with greatest effect. Do you see? The event cropped up in your life and now it is addressed to you. I grant you, it is a surprise, to say the least (a regrettable one as well as comical), that the Greatest Challenge of your existence has taken on the shape and voice of a human worm, and I understand that your greatest wish is to squash it underfoot. But don't you know that heroes *always* have to slay foul-mouthed monsters? Stop complaining about it being not fair just to persuade yourself there's been a mistake. Abandon the notion that the jerk has no place in your life, since the opposite is true. He or she is talking to you, yes, to *you* sir or madam, and now it's time to show your valour.

These considerations require you to redefine both your own position and the operating range you have at your disposal. Destroying the idiot is no longer an issue. He or she existed prior to your noticing, and will no doubt persist in some environment or other in time to come. Your only aim is to stop the lout from doing any harm. But you do grasp that your present task is to determine precisely which board you are playing on, because that is where you will have to find a way of moving the pieces into a new configuration – including in situations where for reasons of social hierarchy you are not in a position to tear strips off your opponent.

So while the idiot is presumably ruining the atmosphere and trampling on what you believe to be important, he or she is *also, and by the same token*, offering you a golden opportunity to show your own worth. You can now make a display of your own intelligence and tactfulness: these qualities have no better use, they become significant only *in relation to* an idiot and *by means of* the idiocy of some other. Human worth would simply have no meaning without these occasional unfortunate encounters where it can be deployed.

Because of the evaluative ambivalence of any event and the reciprocal involvement of subject and object, the occurrence of an idiot in the course of daily life should be seen straight off as a favourable, necessary and welcome opportunity for your own moral development. It's superbly well suited to you and to no one else, since it is happening to you. That's why I now conclude that an idiot is a stroke of luck, and I therefore insist:

3 Be the first to make peace

THE BACKSLIDE BEGINS!

Idiots who would try to impress others with all the factoids they could recall took a bad hit when smartphones came into use. You can now see the poor fools standing all forlorn, looking as stranded as dinosaurs after an Ice Age. Nothing wounds them more gravely than when in mid-conversation about the Middle East or Ming vases their interlocutor whips out the dreaded gizmo and fact-checks on Wikipedia. The spectacle is as sad as watching a threatened species lose another member to a poacher.

Unfortunately, the self-balancing that biologists observe in natural ecosystems comes into play here too. The rolling extinction of idiots who *know stuff* is being accompanied by a corresponding proliferation of idiots who have *been there and done stuff*. Just watch them as they drown you with a list of the towns and countries they've seen, and all the people they know or once knew – and you can see they're having fun! You have to accept that they drape themselves as in a toga with all the power and prestige this gives them, but in fact, they have no need to cover themselves up like that. They dress up warm because they have failed to process their experience and acquaintances into real nourishment; instead, they just want to bury you under an accumulation of raw, undigested junk … They're desperate exhibitionists exposing themselves without opening their raincoats, excruciatingly ashamed of what they persist in *not doing*.

In which the topic of affective excess will be discussed at such depth as to give a highly flattering impression of the author, and of yourself too.

'm sorry, I know you are only half-convinced by the analysis I've just given. Obviously, you have understood the importance of relativising your idea of evil in daily life, a logical operation that has brought the affective spiral to a halt. You have accepted that an idiot is not an evil but only a pain, and that's the terrain where the struggle must happen. Moving on from blaming jerks to picking up the challenge they set, you have refocused your attention, you've stopped thinking about all the time, patience, equanimity, self-confidence and *joie de vivre* that your idiot is wasting, and you are now concentrating on what the jerk is prompting you to invent – namely, ways of demonstrating in the here and now the aforementioned qualities of patience, equanimity and *joie de vivre*.

All the same, I have a lurking suspicion that you are finding it hard to admit that the fuckwit who gave your secrets away or the lout who has lit a barbecue right under your window are offering you genuine *opportunities* for free. I get it, but I'm going to show you why you are wrong. (Please note that I am pursuing this line of thought for my own sake as well, because the jerk I live with, acting quite instinctively and with apparent naivety, seems set on ruining my whole life and, by extraordinary coincidence, is having another stab at it as I write these very words.)

To make any progress at all, we must integrate into our thinking the inevitability of backsliding into emotion. Even the biggest hearts have never managed to shield themselves from it. Once you are familiar with the general principles of moral philosophy (or if you prefer, the path of wisdom), when an idiot runs a red light or dents your bumper and then swears at you for being in the way, your powers of logic vanish into thin air. That too is structural. We may know that almost all our ills are relative and can thus be understood as challenges, and are therefore opportunities for growth in our own lives, but in fact and in practice, it does not turn out like that. Each new test, each annoyance, even if it is utterly trivial (who really cares about scratched bodywork, I ask you?), always presents itself as an *absolute* event and instantly causes us to muddle everything up; and so yet again stupidity makes fools of us all. As I have been saying all along, idiocy will win nearly every time. That alone is a good reason for not surrendering to it!

What I've just described I'd like to refer to from here on as *bedazzlement*. It arises when, due to the impact of an emotion (to be honest, even love and joy can set it off), the number of things you can keep in focus at the same time shrinks in proportion to the strength of the feeling. Like a firework display that blinds you to the rest of the sky, *bedazzlement* turns everything else dark, and the greater your emotion, the less you can see. At each stumbling block, your field of vision undergoes further contraction, and the local event takes on an absolute value, as if nothing before had ever shone as brightly. It would be an understatement to say that your pain stops you thinking. *Bedazzlement* plays a key role in your reluctance to even address a simple word to idiots and jerks, since it constantly brings your mind back to their stupidity.

The impact of emotions and the work they make necessary are mostly not well understood, because a large proportion of philosophers and their descendants tend to use a language of control. I have to concede straight off that they have an excellent point. When a twit drives you to exasperation, or a piece of human scum makes you boil with contempt, you simply have to contain the explosion. You don't do it out of charity, even less for the sake of good manners, but because the eruption set off by the strength of your feeling can wreck what you most value, i.e. it can damage your own interests. Are you going to tell me yet again that it was the fuckwit who lit the fuse? Because that is wrong. The idiot is no more at fault for that than a firework display causes darkness. On the other hand, if you give your emotions a free rein, they can easily do you a lot of harm, and will surely make a bad situation worse.

Because of their explosive potential, emotions appear to us first as forces of disorder; jerks and idiots are also themselves vectors of disorder; ergo, there is great wisdom, as I have said, in urging you to put a leash on your feelings. That is the only means you have for taking control of nitwits – which is what you must do if the universe is to return to what you consider to be its normal state, or, failing that, if you are to get any peace for yourself.

Nonetheless, the notion of control suggests countering the violence of feeling with something like a repressive energy, as if the voice of reason could silence the passions. Thoughtfulness would have to allow you to step back from the immediacy of the event; to control the intensity of lived experience with the cool balm of the mind; to take up an objective position so as to overcome the limitations of subjectivity. There's a lot of good sense in all that, and as is always the case with common sense, it's pretty naive.

All these points share the disadvantage of banking on the dualism of two entities: a stable, unchanging and good order, and a necessarily evil and destructive disorder. The most impatient of my students try to rehabilitate disorder by attributing a positive quality to it. But the problem isn't the value of the two poles, the problem is the dualism itself. Try to be smarter than that. It's not hard to grant that a living order can accommodate disorder, and this means that the ordering principle cannot be contrary to emotion. And, if you grant that the principle cannot be abstracted from emotions, then by implication it must necessarily come from them. To put it another way, a living order presupposes that emotions are capable of self-regulation. In order to explore this interesting idea, we ought to reconsider the ways in which emotions articulate the distinction between the concepts of order and disorder. Here's how.

Let us first posit that the feelings we generally take to be negative ones (fear, sadness, anger and hate) are always fraught with errors and mistakes. However, it does not follow that all such bad feelings boil down to mistaken judgements, that is to say, to purely logical determinations. They can be identified by intense and frequently observable and quantifiable phenomena, such as increased cardiac rhythms, outbreaks of sweating, facial discoloration, tears, and so forth. Consequently, emotions have to be taken as events in themselves, as challenges of a second order. Just like the existence of nitwits and dickheads, the existence of hatred, anger and so on has to be accepted not as a mistake, but as a fact. So you not only have to make do with the existence of the boor who refuses to reward your effort with an acknowledgement that would cost nothing, you also have to survive the feelings he or she arouses in you. To proceed correctly, you have to switch things around. Deal with your own emotions first. Taking care of the idiot comes second.

Now that we have granted emotions the sovereign status of events, we can also assert that they are almost always excessive, and therefore stand on the side of disorder. But on closer inspection, this argument does not stand up. By definition, emotions can only be excessive when they exceed some threshold; if there is a threshold, someone or something must have defined it in advance, irrespective of the emotion; so the very threshold presupposes an instance external to itself. That shows that emotions become excessive whenever (if and only if) an instance of control irritates and exacerbates their sovereign force. Let me explain with an example. You know that it is better not to insult anyone – not even a fuckwit. So the feeling you feel on being up against a human worm naturally clashes with the mental representation that you have of the duty to hold back and which you do not wish to disregard. So the more the energy of your emotion encounters an obstacle, the more violent it becomes. That does not mean you should let go and hurl insults at every idiot in your path, but it does mean you have to find an adequate means of expression for the energy coursing through you, whenever it courses through you.

The main thing is to understand that the immediate association of emotion and disorder, emotion and thought-lessness, emotion and excess, does not derive from the quality of the emotion, but from external interference, such that none of the above (disorder, thoughtlessness, excess) derives directly from the emotion itself. To paint it with a picture: the more screens you put up on the beach to shield you from the wind, the more likely it is that the wind will knock them down. That's not because the wind is intrinsically destructive. Its destructive force comes from the nitwit who puts up screens on a beach.

So instead of blaming your own feelings, you should face the real problem, which is to find an appropriate way of expressing them. What I mean by appropriate is that your words and actions must meet the challenge of *exhausting* the strength of the emotions by draining them entirely, to the bottom of the glass. The expression must also be *appropriate to its environment*, that is to say, put in a form that allows your emotions to be accepted and understood, rather than rejected and denied; and if at all possible, the expression of them should improve the prospects for future interactions. If perchance you find this effort to relieve your feeling and adapt it to circumstances rather conventional and simplistic, that is because you have been reading my proposal from the point of view of an instance of control. I assure you, on the contrary, that you will relieve your heart as you relieve a troubled bowel, and that we'll manage to get the idiots and jerks to lap it all up.

**4 Don't fight feelings
Let them out**

IMPOTENCE
IS THE
FOUNDATION
OF DUTY

Some really ghastly people are simultaneously like elephants and crystal glasses. At first encounter they fill you with a terrifying expectation of risk. From the start, you know you have to tread gently; you step nimbly aside at every turn of phrase, at every eye contact; from one chance meeting to another, you maintain these acrobatics without ever being sure you've done them properly; then one day, it all crashes to the ground. As you contemplate what they've smashed to smithereens, you have an experience of the irreparable – one of the most painful and fascinating of all experiences. Some philosophers, in a spirit of consolation, tell us that the irreparable was basically ineluctable, but that is a gentle fib. The irreparable is usually an accident. That is precisely what defines ghastly people: they make accidents inevitable.

In which it will be shown that the adoption of a moralising posture when faced with an idiot is based on an implicit sermon; that the sermon is a sham; and that a sham cannot give you satisfaction.

Our preceding analyses have allowed us to bring the problem down to its proper size: the challenge of dealing in the here and now with a jerk or a twit who is poisoning your life. The challenge has set your effort in the right direction, which is to say, not counter to your own feelings, but alongside them. Now we may return to the facts, that is to say, to the actions by which idiots dismay you and earn your scorn, so as to determine how to respond to them.

May I first draw your attention most especially to one point: though there do exist beings who are deplorable in all respects, being idiotic – like being wise – is not the essential nature of anybody. What we're dealing with is a form of behaviour. So let's not waste time with word games about 'stupid' being potentially ambiguous as between the designation of a person (*hello, stupid!*) and the quality of an action (*that was stupid!*) or more elaborate and equally insignificant word-matches available in French, English and no doubt other languages besides. Wits may say there is one born every day: but the fact is, nobody is born an idiot, even if there are people whose stupidity seems incorrigible. Consequently, you will concede that doing something stupid and being stupid are one and the same thing. That is why (and this is what interests me) the most common response to stupidity consists of focusing on the act as a separable thing, and of severing the link between what you are – a human being – and what idiots, in doing something idiotic, *are not* but *should be*, to wit, other human beings.

We can therefore assert that the anger that idiots arouse in you is immediately connected to a representation of *duty* or obligation (what *should* be the case). Twits and oafs create a gap between what they do and the way an accomplished human being *ought* to behave, at least in terms of your personal understanding of the human. For the time being, I won't go into the representation or broach the question of how wide the compass of your humanity really is. First I want to shine a light on a particular moralising posture.

A volley of insults, a lengthy improvisational lecture, resentful muttering, silent churning – these reactions to idiots are all actually the same thing. Stupidity in general unleashes considerations which always all boil down to a sermon or a moral teaching. *Are you a jerk or something? That's what I said, you're behaving like an idiot. Stop talking rubbish!* Concise and simple expressions of this kind are masks for different ways of moralising. During an operation that occurs at such speed as to remain unconscious, your mind puts a set of moral duties that you associate with human perfectibility up against an act that does not meet those obligations, and you bash the one with the other like a monkey trying to get a square peg into a round hole. It won't go in. End of story.

However, I will grant you that the attitude that consists

of measuring behaviour against some scale of values and of trying to make others share the underlying system is not entirely absurd. When one person preaches to another, the former is seeking to build on the latter's capacity to understand a number of rules and to accept them as valid, for that is the way idiots may recognise their acts for what they are. If an idiot recognises his or her act as a stupid or improper one, then, by definition, the idiot ceases to be idiotic. In that sense, the tendency to preach is nothing other than an effort to separate idiots (the specific individual, as agent) from their idiocies (as acts). Up to a point, it might be a first step towards reconciliation. As you would like your interlocutors to be supporters and not opponents, and to persuade them to come over to your side, you lay out before them, so to speak, the rules of your side of the world. If they accept them, you will be two human beings facing the same event together.

Preaching is therefore trying to transform what identifies the other. It's a matter of making an idiot disassociate from his or her own act, and identify with the value system you are trying to defend, so that in future the individual who committed an inappropriate act will not do so again. That comes down to saying that you are making an effort to redirect the other's self-construction so as to have him place his action on a scale of values on which, by acknowledging his own error, he will have some catching up to do. As a by-product you understand that only adherence to a *value system* defined in qualitative terms allows quantitative comparisons to be made between people (scoring more or less on the *scale of values*). The main point is that all preaching appeals to an idea of *obligation* that you're trying to get someone who failed to meet it to recognise, in the hope that by recognising her failure she will do better from now on.

But this is where things turn upside down, in quite spectacular fashion. Whoever may be speaking, you realise that the notion of obligation cannot be formulated without taking a strange detour. Of course, in real-life situations, interactions may consist of nothing more than insults. But beneath the simplest expressions there is a machinery of representations that can be brought to light. It doesn't figure in what you actually say to the idiot; we're dealing here with an implicit discourse you are not even aware of, but which could be expressed like this:

You didn't behave as you should have
and it's not me who's telling you, it's more-than-me

Put as a forward projection, the formulation of obligation looks something like this:

You should not behave that way not because I am telling
you

(NB I already failed to avert it)

but because something bigger than me dictates it
(through me)

In the posture I am trying to put into words here, you can see a very curious mixture of projection and smoke-and-mirrors. To begin with, the speaker splits into two entities: the first-person subject of the sentence, but also, alongside that, something else – the law of obligation, speaking through him or her. In other words, the discourse is constructed so as to mask the involvement of the speaker, by attributing the formulated remedy (*you should* or *ought not*) to an outside authority. Why must the preaching posture always refer to something external? Quite simply because the word of the speaker is not enough to establish the utterance as a true obligation. The speaker of such remedies has no authority to utter them, because in the eyes of the interlocutor at this point in the interaction, it is the giver of lessons who is the jerk.

Second, you realise that these kinds of remedies are addressed to hearers who also split into two entities: the one that did in fact mess up, and the imaginary figure of the human being the idiot failed to be.

This analysis allows us to explicate a mechanism of imaginary projections in which the speaker presents herself as a shadow that seems simply to be her double (a conceptual ghost supposedly speaking through her), speaking to another shadow (namely, the human being her interlocutor was not). In brief, it's like having two people standing side by side looking into a mirror: the person I am not, speaking to the one you were not.

But take care! The fact that a sermon presupposes a projection of the self – of an *ideal self*, moreover – onto the other doesn't strike me as particularly problematic. That's because I agree wholeheartedly that humanity would run much better if it consisted exclusively of people like you, and I do mean *you*, my dear reader. I really do believe that! But it seems to me indispensable to identify in the implicit sermon that you give a fundamental trick consisting of two acts of denial. First, when you tell another person what his or her obligations are, you think and speak as if it was not you who were speaking and thinking; you claim to be expressing an unconditional law of obligation, yet it is absurd to think that a human being could formulate a truth without first stating its conditions of validity. Secondly, you treat the idiot's action as if said idiot had already ceased to be a twit. In a nutshell: you are presupposing that you have already achieved what you are still only setting out to do, namely, to change a piece of scum into a human being.

These remarks aren't so difficult to understand. At bottom, the double disjunction I've highlighted (a speaker, 'I', saying that it's 'not I' who is speaking, about an object (you) who is not what you are) gives clear expression to one thing. Once you adopt the preacher's posture, yelling insults and giving lectures boil down to the same thing: you are trying to say something that you are not managing to say, that you cannot say, and that you are therefore saying in an abominable, muddled, non-specific and aberrant way, and you would need well-honed skills in informal logic to see through it all. So all there is to understand is this: anyone who preaches to others is implicitly giving an authentic, personal confession of impotence. A giver of moral lessons invokes the absolute and the whole of humanity only because for and by himself he cannot say what he means in a manner that is satisfactory to him and to his interlocutor.

As a result, moral discourse – preaching – is actually the theme tune of the Great Panic from which we have been trying to escape. I call it a *tune* because the words of the song are almost entirely devoid of meaning. Confronted with a worm or another creepy-crawly, you suffer to such a degree that your power of expression is halved, turns back on itself, and blurts out plain nonsense: *I am not saying what I am saying*, which can be glossed as an outlandish way of saying: *I'm at a loss, you turd, have pity on me.*

Insofar as it involves a posture that consists of remaining tangled, silent and speechless in one's own voice, a sermon purely and simply expresses an appeal for help. But that's completely crazy! You're asking your opponent for help! And you're doing it by sabotaging your own capacity for expression! What nightmare have you dragged us into? My friends, I beseech you: Wake up!

5 **Don't preach
Stop judging
Right now!**

HOW MORAL AUTHORITIES CONFLICT WITH EACH OTHER

Telephone service lines allow us to experience powerlessness very vividly indeed. After waiting for ages and going from one prompt to another – press 1, press 0, press 4, press the hash key – you get to tell some low-wage, low-security employee about a problem that floors him, either because he's not had the right training, or because he is authentically powerless. That's when your humiliation by things (which is in fact a permanent state of being, called 'real life') turns in on itself and then into *anger* at being powerless, which is basically a kind of shame. Meanwhile, as the guy on the line tries to sell you a package deal or a special offer, your sincerest desire is to strangle the poor fool with the telephone wire.

All in all, like a rabid dog or fox trying to pass on the infection, the phone guy has dug his teeth into you at a place that makes both of you impotent. That's how communication companies, in a show of cruelty that nobody else would dare to give, throw us back into the phenomenon they are supposed to overcome, namely, incommunicability. Like all PR efforts, these 'customer service lines' are designed not so much to sort your problem as to stifle it, until after the next billing cycle.

In which we shall study the conflict of authority into which idiots draw us, and how to soften its sting.

By their sheer obstinacy, idiots have managed to make us stumble into the fundamental principles of moral philosophy. Don't worry – one of the proofs that you are not an idiot yourself is that you appreciate the joy of thought. So even if your path is going to get steeper and have you scratching your head, I am confident you will tolerate what counts as pleasure in philosophy, which consists, in the main, of attacking your own conceptual defences, charging through the breach thus made, and discovering a new horizon.

So take a look at the following hypothesis (I don't consider it has been proven yet): that the way we preach to jerks and nitwits, explicitly or not, is the howling anthem of our own impotence. By extension, the idea of a moral obligation applying to them could be no more than the projection onto them (onto idiots, that is) of our inability to see ourselves in the astounding stupidity they brandish as their flag. In a word, any sermon could be saying implicitly:

I can't get you to act as I want you to, so I am telling you that you ought

You'll presumably object that I should not badmouth morality like that. Moral principles make it possible to live together, and we wouldn't get anywhere unless we held some values to be absolute. Or else, you'll take the other side, and say we can easily dispense right now with blind and pointless blaming, because we'll never get anywhere if we allow norms to block spontaneity and innovation. But your take on moral principles is quite irrelevant to my point. I am not yet looking at moral principles as such; I'm talking about an interaction in which a human being adopts (if only implicitly) a particular *moralising posture* towards another human being – something that, rightly or wrongly, good parents and good friends always do, but so do ill-mannered birdbrains.

In this context, the notion of obligation appears to be a linguistic operator intended to prompt action in the absence of other motives, that is to say by obscuring the relationship between the interlocutors, by masking the agents in the situation, and by giving no place to any articulation between the wishes of the two parties – which is the ultimate means of robbing the interaction of all that could make it a productive one.

It may be the case that this posture has no rational foundation, but for the moment I would like to show that what matters is that it is ineffective. Reread this formulation as if it was being said to you by an oaf:

> *This just can't go on, not because I'm telling you but because something other than I is telling you*

That makes no impact on you at all. You let the preacher preach on without really listening, you don't grant the sermon one gram of truthfulness, its words have no more purchase on you than the fibs of a compulsive liar. As a result, you have to admit that the sermon is an insufficient response to a real problem. The problem consists in the fact that both interlocutors have lost confidence in the other's capacity to formulate anything true or receivable. This is the absolutely crucial point. Idiots, because they are idiots, saw off the branch of the tree on which language sits. More precisely, a cog in the machinery of human interaction has jammed. The outage disables the elementary rules of verbal exchange, making social intercourse impossible.

Moralising discourse can get you round this problem, but only once. It claims that what you are saying does not depend on you; idiots can therefore accept the moral lesson, even if they have no confidence at all in the person speaking it, namely you. For there is a moral law; it exists; it was not invented by me; and it forbids such and such behaviour. On closer inspection, the way in which the moralising posture masks the speaker's involvement in what he or she says is rather clever; for obfuscation is essential to re-establish communication between two beings who don't want to listen to each other.

So why then does it work so badly? Because moral authority is no more than a hypothesis, it is a mere shadow of what has been lost, namely, reciprocal confidence between interlocutors. That's why this kind of authority is useless. Idiots don't want to know about what you're trying to put over on them with your argument – and they don't understand a word of it anyway. So the crisis of confidence turns into a conflict of authority, and the conflict of authority becomes a conflict of interpretation. Despite its cloak of dignity and virtue, your sermon has in the end done nothing more than shift the problem to a different terrain, without resolving it in any way.

Indeed, if your interlocutor is endowed with speech (most idiots are, unfortunately) then he or she will be thoroughly inclined to return the favour and to reply to you with a sermon of his or her own. And even if you are prepared to recognise a difference between good and bad, and even if you grant that a desirable way of regulating human behaviour exists, you are not going to let an oaf of that kind give you a moral lesson, since in this instance the oaf is trampling on it.

But there's worse to come. Real fuckwits – people who are not and never will be your friends – possess a value system that is different from yours. In their view, the behaviour you consider unacceptable is perfectly OK, and it's the way *you* behave that is beyond the pale. That's the hardest, the most abysmal, the least tolerable of all the truths that this book has to reveal: human beings are not always idiots by accident, by chance, by lack or excess, by circumstance or without intending to be fools. Some people are *systematically stupid*.

I am sorry that the fates have given me the task of revealing this truth, but since we all suffer from it, we might as well look things in the face. What is generally called *otherness* does not only refer to the physical, linguistic and cultural differences that enrich the human race. Otherness also means that in all societies and in all social strata there are beings – and not just single cases, for they even have friends who agree among themselves – who don't care about coherence. Instead of having a value system that is different from yours, which would be interesting in itself, what they value is the absence of logic, that is to say, incoherence. Those are the people I call systematic idiots. If you doubt their existence (as I did until recently), I am able to introduce you to someone who is neither stupid nor mad, and not even nasty, who is brilliant at his job (real jerks are often not unsmart). This real gem – the purest specimen I have had the opportunity of getting to know – *does not want* to understand, despite having the means of doing so; or in other words, he *perseveres heroically* in his own stupidity.

So the great difficulty encountered by moralising discourse addressed to any random lout or twit is that it presupposes a minimal common ground as a basis for discussing how to evaluate our respective behaviours. But unlike children and more generally people connected to us by ties of affection, nincompoops have no reason to accept your value system, or to make the effort to understand it so as to question it. A person who refuses even the notion of setting rules together makes mutual understanding impossible, and plunges everyone into a situation of complete powerlessness.

Why do blockheads not want to negotiate? Because they do not grant you any kind of authority. But, you ask me, why do they still say no to bowing to the higher authority of reason, each of us alongside the other, as equals?

I can see you don't understand. Idiots don't want you. They have no respect for you, that's clear, but in addition, they don't even want to acknowledge your existence. They have no *consideration* for you. What they most want is to pretend you don't exist at all, or, more precisely, that your existence and all that it implies by way of wishes, thoughts, hopes, fears, anxious queries and suppressed feelings, the whole world of emotions, signs and images that lie just beneath your outward appearance, has no relevance to them whatsoever. In their eyes, you are null and void. This posture is so stupid, and so profoundly insulting, that it takes you aback, but you have to admit once and for all that it exists. Co-humanity between you and your jerk has collapsed, and I'd go so far as to say that co-existence has also fallen into a black hole. I have undergone this experience right here, under my own roof, and it is no exaggeration to say that it opened up before my eyes one of the most vertiginous chasms in my whole life.

This catastrophe drains away any effort to establish even the appearance of a dialogue, for it nullifies all confidence between your idiot and you, and even any common desire. So there's no question of negotiating, because there is no translation possible between these two worlds. That is why authority (the authority of reason, morality, God or whatever absolute you choose) conflicts with itself. It may well be a desperate attempt to prompt a switch, but it collapses in the course of the interaction. In any case, when you preach to a blockhead, you're speaking a dialect that's not understood. Because of the constraints and indeterminacies of human language, there's no end to misapprehensions even between people of good will, but in a moment of crisis with a jerk, incommunicability reaches down to an unfathomable depth.

I'm sorry to say that this is not the end of it. Interactions are not only linguistic. They draw on a whole range of sense impressions (tone of voice, manual and facial gestures, physical posture and appearance, gut feelings (and the feeling in your gut) as well as reminders of past experiences, and so on). Each of us interprets these signals in our own way, which are variable and often contradictory. This overarching sign system means that the direction people go when they lose their feeling of co-humanity is impossible to foresee and out of anyone's control. I write this with some trepidation: under these conditions, a jerk or an idiot may do anything at all.

Let me add that it seems to me to be useful to remember that the interactional pathologies that suppress mutual understanding, and therefore the confidence we have in other people, and therefore the authority that we recognise, do not simply boil down to misapprehensions of symbolic language. There is also an ungraspable realm of affinities and hostilities between any two humans (you can label them as spiritual, chemical, pheromonal, or whatever else) which means that you possess something which jerks *can't stand*, something that needles them, maybe even attacks them before you've moved your little finger or said a word. The feeling is most frequently mutual.

You may not like the sound of my voice; your way of scratching yourself may not be my cup of tea; but you and

I can still listen to each other. With dickheads and dolts, it's different. Like a tidal flow, idiots try all they can to make you submit to their pseudo-systems by destroying yours; and precisely because that is the language they speak (if you can call it a language) or more usually hiss or bellow, etc., they provoke you, irritate you, and shock you by all means available – and even, on occasions, go on and on, pontificating about the meaning of life.

At the present time, we have no choice but to recognise this fact: if there is a conflict between authorities, it is clearly and plainly because empathy has been lost, and without empathy the conditions for restoring it are not to be found. This interactional catastrophe sinks our common humanity to the ocean floor. Is the jerk still moving his jaw? Maybe we've now reached the point where we should listen to what's being said.

**6 Stop playing with words
Idiots don't *want* to understand**

Some of them go over the top

'That's wrong!'

'What do you mean, that's wrong?'

'I'm telling you it's wrong! It's wrong! It's just not true!'

Others don't even care

'No big deal. Whatever. Comes to the same thing.'

Idiots aren't all the same, but they are idiots just the same.

In which you will learn how to listen to idiots, and even how to make them talk so as to de-escalate conflicts. And also how to talk back.

Time for a recap. When a jerk or an idiot appears in your life, they do so by means of actions or utterances that plainly exhibit their stupidity. Your attention then focuses on the individual event. When you think about the event (generally speaking, you think about it *a bit too much*), all your human attributes – your heart, your rational mind, your gut and the hair that bristles on the back of your neck – tell you that the action or utterance is something that another human being *should not* have done, at least not in the situation in which it occurred. At the same time, you feel the moral values that you wish to share asserting themselves within you. The (implicit or explicit) sermon that you then provide is thus an appeal for these criteria to be recognised. However, on closer inspection, this appeal is a wail of impotence, since it takes for granted (unwittingly, to be sure) conditions that are precisely those that have been forfeited by the idiot's action. Of course, we can allow that the sermon aims at attracting your idiot's attention so that he or she behaves in future with greater care and greater awareness of the (moral, political, economic, ecological, etc.) consequences of his or her actions. But there are many other ways of encouraging others to do *this* and *not that*.

This should certainly persuade you not to engage in moralising when faced with a jerk or idiot – I will come back to this point later. For the moment, I want to observe how it allows you to remain calm and unperturbed when someone tries to lecture you. The most common reaction, which is both natural and entirely ineffective, is to try to deny that you have committed the *fault* that your preacher seeks to lumber you with (as you must surely know, idiots love to make others feel guilty). However, any attempt to justify your own actions involves such a phenomenal number of mistakes that I won't even bother to list them. But you must accept at least this truth: as you blurt out your self-justification, you simply don't know which system of values to invoke – your own, or the idiot's. You assimilate (or pretend to assimilate) the system that the jerk seeks to impose on you, whereas, in actual fact, systematic idiots *do not have* a system, since they don't give a fig for coherence! So do not justify yourself: it is humiliating and pointless and can even be dangerous (for how will you ever forgive the ninny for having forced you to justify yourself?). Though I do spy a grain of generosity in your attempt, it is above all essential for you to learn how to *deny that the idiot is competent* to judge the case. Unless you start out by trampling the judgements of idiots and oafs underfoot, you will never get out of the woods.

Instead of engaging with them, you should instead be aware of the fact that people who preach at you are in reality just bewailing their own powerlessness. The blockheads are trying to get you to recognise their capacity to inspire confidence at the very point where they have lost it (actually, you have both lost it when the interaction capsized). Their utterances are no more than lamentations. To hear them right, you have to void them of all prescriptive content (which nothing requires you to recognise, since the lessons can only derive authority from you) and strip them of the blame they cast (since blaming is only the preacher's way of projecting their shame onto you), and then receive the lamentation – yes, receive it, welcome it and accept it as testimony of a pain that asks only to be recognised.

Basically, when preachers tie themselves in knots by appearing to say *you should not be hurting me*, they are really only saying *it hurts*. Alright! So forget the first words in such sentences and stay clear of the trap of answering that it wasn't your fault but theirs. Just blank out the 'shoulds' and 'oughts', and bend your ear to the moaning. If you've followed this analysis from the start, you know already that the aim of sermons *always was* to obtain recognition. However, though you may have thought that the aim was to make you recognise that a mistake has been made (which is the very principle of shame and repentance), it turns out that recognising the *reason for speaking* and the *reason for acting* are much more important than debates over *whose fault* it was.

If we follow this thread, we can find a way of being immune to the deceptions of the universalising discourse that underpins a great number of the conflicts we have with jerks and dumbasses. Sermons are generated by an escape into generalities (that is to say, by induction) that is directly connected to the way the interaction has capsized. As I've shown, this strategy does not restore any of what has been lost, since instead of convincing your opponent, you just speechify around the very confidence that is missing. That's why preachers ask their listener to recognise authority – in order to restore confidence. But since they do so while masking the subject in whom confidence really needs to be had (namely, themselves), they are going to have a hard time restoring anything at all. And if they're in conflict with a champion fuckwit, they'll never manage it.

The vicious circle of lesson-giving, centred on irrecoverably lost confidence, can only ever be broken by recognising the sermon as a funeral chant lamenting an interaction that has hit a brick wall.

Consequently, if you just manage to hear the plea for recognition that underlies preaching, you will escape the preacher's false effect of authority, which is a true discourse of powerlessness. From the strict point of view of discourse, that means that the resolution of our conflicts with screwballs, deplorables and nutcases of the same ilk should be thought of not in terms of judgements (generating theoretical propositions such as *Socrates is an idiot*) but in terms of *stories* by means of which the genesis of representations and wishes can be reconstructed as a narrative. In taking this step, we have struck upon the kind of discourse that ought to bring relief from emotions – the bonehead's emotions, and yours as well. The fundamental issue is storytelling. Only a story can assuage the conflict: a story allows the truth to emerge at the intersection of different points of view, making it unnecessary to reach agreement (as is necessary in a discourse of concepts) and allowing also for imprecision and the absence of certainty.

What's more, the absolute privilege of storytelling in human interaction is one of the most beautiful things we can observe in the world. When you have learned to acknowledge suffering, to hear it and to encourage its expression, what you will then learn is this: the sermons that are dumped on you will lose their main power (which is to get on your nerves), and the people who dump them on you will progressively lose their accusing tone and drift into a confession which will give them relief. Now if such jerks want to be in the right, they almost certainly won't lie to you. They'll be sincere in the story they tell you, so as to show that they are in the right. Telling another person about yourself in that way is not communicating, it is at a deep level an *action* undertaken *in common*.

From that point of view, what I called *bedazzlement* – the way an event that arouses a strong emotion stops us from thinking – is not resolved, as philosophers like to believe, by a switch of the mind that illuminates obscure issues and explains the behaviour and utterances of fools and oafs by identifying their causes. We can only vanquish the bedazzlement that human stupidity engenders by renouncing conceptualisation once and for all (that is to say, by not making judgements), and by putting all our trust in the power of storytelling. That's right! Because then you don't have to accept the version of facts that idiots provide; at a pinch, you don't even have to understand everything they tell you. Don't forget that a musical melody provides a narrative thread in which there is absolutely nothing to understand. The main thing to remember is that whenever an idiot arises in your life, all you can do is to give up on communication in the classical sense (and in particular, conceptual communication). The most efficient strategy is to open an emergency confession booth. Idiots are in pain, dammit! Even if their language is not yours, let them tell you where it hurts. Admittedly, doing so is a bit disgusting and deadly boring, and you certainly have no natural wish to come to the aid of the intellectually challenged. And nobody – and certainly not a prize idiot – is asking you to sort out their problems for them. On the other hand, by listening to their complaint and encouraging them to tell you what they want you to hear, you will end up achieving your aim, which is to restore elementary trust, and to make your own life easier.

You will perhaps object that idiots and jerks, who have already made us relativise moral standards, are now on the brink of making us give up truth as well. Letting numbskulls tell us their stories, well, maybe ... but at what price? Now that is a real philosopher's objection. Once again, the point treats truth in propositional terms (for instance: *Shirley is a twerp*, or else, *Socrates is not an idiot*) and you suppose that these propositions must be either true or false. That understanding of truth derives from the law of the excluded middle, but that law is too strict to apply in the moral sphere (not to mention the fact that modern logic abandoned it long ago). To cut a long story short, I can say this: two people do not need to be in complete agreement to make truth together, because the truth of moral situations comes from the overlap in their respective positions. To approach that truth absolutely requires us to incorporate into it the opinion of the most benighted of idiots or the most dishonest of oafs, so as to determine with them from what angle their views are in some part sharable and can therefore be made compatible with the views of others. The labour of such incorporation, also known as diplomacy, is one of the great challenges of our times (maybe of all times, but I wasn't there).

This incorporation is also at the heart of our relationship to emotions. It can indeed be said that any emotion is relieved by being spoken aloud, and exacerbated by recourse to theory. The labour of opening up and listening to storytelling allows us to meet the challenge of our emotions as well as the challenge of the emotions of idiots and jerks. So tell your own story, too! You can't avoid it. Unburden yourself of your feelings. But you must absolutely not ask idiots to acknowledge the authenticity of your pain; you should seek that support elsewhere, from people of good will and good sense. (We learned a while back that idiots don't give a toss for the truth and that they're not looking for it in any case.) You will be just like them for as long as you try to impose it on them in a theoretical way. The great moral challenge is not to make idiots more intelligent but to achieve something more modest: to prevent them from doing harm *in practice*.

Recourse to theory brooks one exception, however, and it is called philosophy. Indeed, just as storytelling is not something that only writers do, but an indispensable part of human interactions (as I have just demonstrated), so too is philosophy not principally an academic enterprise. Insofar as it relies on conceptualisation, philosophy is the name of a process that comes into play every time some emotion that you have takes the form of a wish to understand it, which in turn bursts into words that start to articulate it in abstract concepts (as I am doing here). Manipulating the concepts as they lose their direct connection to immediate experience constitutes a new experience in itself, and it becomes a veritable exploration of states of mind of the third degree (the first degree is awareness of the event, the second is awareness of the emotion aroused by it). In that sense, the Heavenly Vault of Ideas in which we move is nothing other than the celestial mirror of our guts, which we pour out among our civilised friends, in forms as subtle and refined as a single malt, until our thirst is quenched.

7 **Share your stories**
Encourage others to tell theirs

WHY THE
POWERS THAT
BE DON'T
GIVE A DAMN

On questions they call political or religious, twits hold views with the firmness of a handyman's vice. Convictions bring strength, calm and stability to most people, but to blockheads they bring a phenomenal degree of fragility. When they scream out loud at the slightest reservation or the tiniest objection you might want to express, they sound as injured as if you had pulled out a fingernail with pliers.

In such occurrences, a simple recourse is to cut the sound. Politics and religion share the characteristic of being concepts of an *exclusively* practical nature: your acts show what kind of citizen you are, just as they demonstrate what kind of believer you may be. Once you've switched off the soundtrack and let the acts be what they are, the unbelievable nonsense that human beings churn out about 'God' (without even wondering what they are talking about) or 'the authorities' (ditto) becomes as puffy as clouds drifting across a clear blue sky, beneath which you are free to come and go as you please.

In which a reflection on laws shows two different ways of fighting against the idiocy of institutions.

The preceding chapters present several ideas that go against the grain, up to a point. To wit: appealing to moral duty in daily life is, for the main part, a lamentation; what it bewails is the loss of trust; and reciprocal attention to the stories told is the best, if not the only, way to overcome such loss.

If I go by my experience as a teacher of philosophy, propositions of this kind usually divide the audience in two. Some listeners leave the classroom feeling satisfied and happy to play around with the new idea, to see what it can do; others, usually my favourite students, find the idea perfectly arbitrary and even inadequate. Teaching relies both on the more or less warranted support of students who take my ideas on board (and without whom teaching would be unbearable), and on the more or less justified demands of students who resist them. That's how we make progress through the semester.

In my analysis of the moralising posture, where I reduced preaching to a plea for recognition, I conscientiously avoided discussing whether or not louts and idiots were responsible for their own stupidity (that is to say, for the stupidity of their actions) and I did not even broach the question as to who has the better grounds for appealing to the authority of moral law. On the contrary, I restricted myself to a relativistic approach, because I wanted to show that *situations* allow us to isolate specific problems about the use of speech, and therefore about how precisely to listen to moral discourse, and why such discourse is infinitely less effective than storytelling.

I now want to do justice to those readers who were not convinced by my arguments because they had in mind from the start situations where they were in the right. I can only agree wholeheartedly that when you are faced with a sadist trampling on his subordinates or a flibbertigibbet who won't take responsibility for anything, you tell yourself – as I tell myself – that you have every right to fight back, because you are defending something worth fighting for. On such occasions, it's not a matter of striving towards general human perfectibility. The issue is simply enforcing respect of a specific right that is perfectly clear in your mind. On the other hand, the term 'right', though it is easy to use, refers to a very heavy concept; to be more precise, to a field in which few things are obvious or cut-and-dried.

I might as well warn you that we are going to launch an assault on a rather mighty fortress. But if you have soldiered on this far, you may have noticed that these considerations, although they are abstract – and precisely because they are abstract – allow us to make a step towards refining our sensibilities and improving our behaviour.

Let the given be one of the millstones that are the object of our investigation – a yahoo or an excrement in respect of whom you reckon you are *in the right*. Please note that being *in the right* is not a state of being. It is a claim. If you believe that you are within your rights when standing in line in the same way you are a mammalian biped, then you have to grant that daily life among humans normally proceeds on that basis, and that therefore we are all within our rights in almost every action we take – breathing, coughing, being stupid, etc. So you must also grant that any human life unfolds, so to speak, and without it being noticed, in the realm of rightfulness. And you will acknowledge, as I do, that the only interesting cases are those where the facts of the matter do not match up with what is right. So let us agree that 'being in the right' does not describe the state I am in when I am cooking; it designates the state I claim to be mine when I ask my flatmate (oy vey!) to clean up the kitchen after a party. A request that he treats as a fascist onslaught.

There are three kinds of cases in which the claim to be 'in the right' may arise, and each is problematic in its own way:

1. Your claim requires the introduction of a law that does not exist, but which would provide a better fit with the facts.
2. You remind someone they are infringing existing laws that are perfectly clear.
3. You demand respect of some moral duty that will never be explicitly required by the law.

Pillocks and boneheads, as you well know, have an unrivalled talent for locating loopholes in the law as efficiently as a perfect gas. Not all of them are law-breakers. Some of them are legalistic opportunists who cleverly exploit the blind spots in the system while staying within the letter of the law. I'll come back later to the topic of these so to speak super-adapted idiots, but for now, let's investigate the three kinds of cases in which you consider them *not* to be in the right when you are quite sure that you *are*. As we shall see, not the tiniest sliver of the social space is immune from disruption by fools and oafs. They may not know why or how they are doing so, but that doesn't make them think of stopping. For your entertainment, and with all due respect, let us begin with idiots who hold office in public employment.

Why start with officials? Because they are the limbs and organs of government, and because governments are the mothers of all institutions set up by positive laws. In other words, governments set up the kinds of organisations that are authorised by written legislation and intended to structure ways of life by means of regulations and the allocation of resources. Without yet broaching legal issues, I would like to point out that since our ways of living are in constant flux, it is structurally imperative for public institutions to be in a permanent process of reform. As a result, all institutions, though they may appear to be fixed and stable, constitute an evolutionary reality and are always playing catch-up with changing customs, ideas, cultures, and so forth.

This brief reminder is all we need to understand a whole range of stupidities. By definition, dear friends, institutions never work properly, since they are theoretically *stable* forms intended to give structure to a *changing* reality; they define *singular* norms intended to shape *multiple* realities; so that institutions and the laws that define them must constantly be corrected, reformed or modified so as to improve their fit with the real lives of human beings and their relationships with non-humans (animals, forests, machines, and even minds, mathematical operations, and so on). Since governmental and inter-governmental organisations are always in a process of rebuilding themselves, by virtue of the fact that History is always several lengths ahead of them, officialdom remains as idiotic today as it was in Hammurabi's Babylon. Whatever adjustments you desire with all your heart, and which may (or may not) come about, officialdom will be just as idiotic in ten thousand years' time when the Targaryen hold the Throne. That will not be much comfort to anyone, but if you think in terms of the next twenty thousand years you may be a little more patient as you wait for your turn to speak to an official.

That is why you must not blame the officials, but the institutions, for being weak in the head. Institutions are always structurally ill-matched to concrete situations. Bureaucracy, moreover, has made the phenomenon more acute. It places on government employees ever more soul-destroying tasks, and undermines the conditions which would make it possible for workers to feel involved and to draw some modest satisfaction from their work. Bureaucracy submits officials to forms of life that simply wear them out, thus adding a layer of surliness to the structural malfunction of the system itself. This should remind us that our moods and mental operations do not take place in the privacy of our minds (as I keep telling you), but express and shape situations and relationships that can be analysed through lenses of different powers of magnification. Sociologists have the task of revealing the social conditions under which idiots are created. My task is to formulate conceptual tools that anybody can use in situations where they have the good luck to encounter a swine in the flesh.

Consequently, you have every right to bemoan the stupidity of institutions, and to say that the powers that be don't give a damn for you or for me, because that is entirely correct. Ministries and departments are constantly retooling, but are never quite fit for purpose, so citizens have to struggle in order to assert their rights, which is to say, to obtain recognition for the legitimacy of a society's demand to have a framework that fits the people of which it is composed – especially those who are outside that society's formal framework of rights. For instance, there aren't full legal frameworks for undocumented migrants or the utterly destitute, but as *de facto* members of society they are entitled as much as anyone else to request modification of the law. At the same time, and for the same reasons, public employees must constantly struggle to stop the ever-crumbling state apparatus from chewing them up (unless it is already too late, as for a school principal I can think of – but let's not go there).

These remarks allow us to distinguish between two equally legitimate but very different reactions that you may have when you are up against the idiocy of public institutions. On the one hand, the posture of *revolt* against their structural stupidity is indispensable in a democracy: without the commitment of all and every one of us to solving collective problems, we would quickly find ourselves living under a *de facto* tyranny. To be honest, I have to admit that the increasing apathy of individuals and their withdrawal from public life has brought us near to that point already. It is therefore essential that you continue to rebel against institutional mindlessness, and never stop letting it upset you.

On the other hand, political revolt cannot remain only the voice of emotion if it is to have any effect on making laws. It becomes a political programme only if it seeks to latch on to existing institutions. In other words, people who support a programme have to be able and willing to work with their opponents – to work together in a constructive frame of mind with real oafs and actual idiots, the very people who are the most active in politics and in charge of all kinds of public and private institutions (I'll show later on why idiots get to be in charge of everything). Indeed, since political skill consists in making different forces converge without collapsing into idiocy, you can deduce that politics cannot fail to tumble into it, since it is logically self-contradictory to *always* solve *all* conflicts for the good of *all* (in particular, though *this is only one part of the problem*, when you are working on behalf of some and not others).

These remarks will, I hope, make you more determined and also more patient in your interactions with the tumbledown edifices of institutions. They were already a great annoyance to citizens in Antiquity; and I can guarantee that when you enter into conflict with them, *you are in the right*. But there is a difficulty when it comes to defining the forms of political activism that are effective and pertinent to claiming your rights. In fact, it seems to me that the advantages of striving to remain within the law are so great that it would be hard to give up on it. The advantages are these: to bring within the logic of law, and to put under government protection, beings and situations that were previously outside them, with consequences that were at best absurd, and at worst inhuman. Unfortunately, the extension of the realm of law – introducing a law that does not exist, but which would provide a better fit with the facts, the first of the three cases we outlined at the start of this chapter – has a very serious drawback. Since it is the same stumbling block as in the second kind of cases in which the claim to be 'in the right' may arise (where you remind someone they are infringing existing laws, decrees and legal judgements), I propose to keep it for the next chapter. For the moment, if you have coped with this chapter, please remember this lesson:

8 **Respect your opponents, and your struggle will become political**

WHY THREATS ARE A FORM OF SUBMISSION

In hierarchical organisations, one of the most widespread forms of idiocy is to require others to work harder and/or to overwork, without stopping to ask what the purpose of the extra work would be, or what benefit it might bring to make it worthwhile.

Overwork, a variant of stupidity bordering on hysteria, serves only to drain the meaning from the work that you do and to darken its shadow – the idiotic flabbiness of people who don't give a damn.

In which it will be learned that an appeal to the law may be a way of making a threat; and that such threats express a desire for submission.

In order to face up to idiots with the best weapons we can muster, we must first have a glance at the philosophy of law. The aim of this detour is to clarify the concept of authority. We need that clarification not in order to get idiots to understand it (they understand nothing, because they do not *want* to), but so as to have a better grasp of our own legitimacy, which increases our chances of overcoming the fools and jerks in our lives.

Among the three kinds of cases where people can justifiably say they are 'in the right', the first showed that citizens can legitimately act to ensure that a real situation occurs within the law even if the organs of the state (the government, its departments, the police, and so forth) drag their feet. Your membership of the social body grounds your legitimacy with respect to institutions, and you can therefore act not just *in the name of all*, but *as one among all*. Society is perpetually up against the stupidity of institutions that it never ceases to form and reform, and which in turn shape society. Faced with such stupidity, you could choose to do nothing at all, but that is rationally indefensible, since institutions by definition do not work properly, and so in some way always challenge and defy you.

I now wish to study cases of the second kind, where assholes make light of existing law with all the alacrity of sausage dogs shitting on the front lawn right under your nose. These cases look straightforward enough. If there is a law that forbids such and such a behaviour, then it means that there is a penalty for said behaviour. So the fact that you thought or told yourself 'I am within my rights' when you were up against a ghastly lady with a little dog, a pickpocket, or a crook who hacked into your bank account, means that you have the backup of a rule of behaviour that has the force of law: the difference between a rule and a law being precisely that a law rests on force.

In theory, at least, the force of the state is no joke. It can strike your wallet (by means of a fine), and it can constrain your body (by means of imprisonment). Although this may look only like a collateral effect, it makes public both the crime and the punishment, giving recognition to the suffering of the victim (that is one of the basic functions of justice), and helping perpetrators acknowledge their acts for what they are (the one and only function of the penalty, which is *not* revenge). However, extending the domain of law has a serious downside. Any increase in the number of laws paves the way for the state to encroach further on private life, and that is not good news: government should only intervene when there is no other option. In the second place, increasing numbers of laws tends to accustom you to appealing to legal process, in other words to the big-machine-that's-tougher-than-you-are-you-stupid-oaf, instead of using other means to resolve conflicts –

and paradoxically, that is an even more undesirable consequence.

The law adapts to changes in society, whereas society changes in response to developments of many different kinds (in technology, in the environment, trade, ideas, arts, etc., *as well as laws*). All power relationships are therefore located in very complex networks of actions and reactions. That means that the agents of the authority of the state are not so much law enforcement officials as the citizens themselves, when without realising the advantages and disadvantages of thinking this way, they conceptualise the power relationships that hold between themselves as existing under a 'threat from above'. Unfortunately, people who are lucky enough to live in a society that respects the rule of law naturally develop a tendency to want to have a law for every aspect of life. This tendency fosters a steady increase in the way governments encroach on individual life – and an omnipresent state is the definition of totalitarianism.

That's how our attempt to deal with idiots has turned us into slaves. We've made ourselves unable to manage without rule-giving institutions. Outside the realm of government, general social structures, including markets and networks, also have the status of institutions, because they too produce rules of discourse and behaviour that shape interactions between human beings. But when the representation of some Normative Authority has become integral to all our interactions, we will have managed to create a totalitarian system without needing a dictator to do it for us.

Should we conclude that it would be better to avoid extending the domain of law? No, because extensions of the law define improvements in public institutions, and therefore in the conditions of social life. But to avoid totalitarianism, every additional law requires – as compensation and as an accompaniment, so to speak – every citizen to acquire additional autonomy: to learn the skill of solving problems *without regard* for the law, or, better still, *before* being obliged to call on the forces of law and order. The engine of totalitarianism is not simply the extension of the domain of law; it consists more in the manner in which, by observing the rules, we attempt to impose them on others.

Now, let us have a think. With all due respect to worshippers of law and order, we have to admit that most of the time, the state does *not* settle our disputes, or else does so only *at very high cost*. In theory, the force of law is very efficient and forceful – it can involve trained officers with firearms, who are certainly needed on occasion to head off jerks and idiots and prevent them going into action when they prove to be criminal. But in practice, the implementation of the force of law is neither simple nor automatic. Quite the opposite. Most thickheads are well aware of the fact, and exploit it. The swine who sexually harasses you is certainly guilty of a punishable offence, but in order to assert the right that you have under the law, you have to undertake immensely burdensome legal proceedings that progress at an inhumanly slow speed. For the state is a very, *very* big-machine-that's-tougher-than-you-are-you-stupid-oaf. It is absolutely necessary that the procedure exists; but resorting to it is not something you may ever want to do.

Although there is a fundamental distinction to be made between incivility and a misdemeanour, and although queue-jumping and groping a junior colleague have nothing to do with each other, the victims of both these actions – who are in the right, and blameless too – are unfortunately in similar situations. They are utterly on their own, they are powerless and without support. Their dismay is above all a collective failure. It shows that it is a *far, far better thing* to acquire the skills necessary to stop such offences from arising, and if possible, to mete out 'punishment' (that is to say, to create awareness) at micro-level. It is indispensable to encourage and cultivate a form of social awareness that remains alive in every individual, who thus becomes capable of interacting with boors and dickheads at an informal and so to speak infra-legal level. Laws, judges and police officers can and should carry on providing a ring-fence for criminals, but beyond making new laws, we must be able to solve our conflicts as far as possible without resorting to the institutions of the state.

Reciprocally, and now with all due respect to the simplest kind of anarchists, power relations are primarily located in the mental representations and actual practices of all and every one of us. So one of the roles of institutions (I'm not saying they play these roles well) is, paradoxically, to *protect* citizens from indulging in their constant obsession with subjecting their conflicts to authority, which is in fact a deep tendency towards submission. Yes indeed, despite it being a political symptom of some gravity, submission is a natural tendency of human (and not only human) beings. Where does it come from? That's no mystery.

It's a fact that we do not have *no reason* for our theoretically perverse inclination towards submission. Submission commends itself to us as an exit strategy from powerlessness, or more precisely, as a way of bringing an end to the dismay (or anxiety, or shame – everyone has a different way of reacting) that we feel when we become aware of our own impotence – what I shall call from now on our *insufficiency*. An interactional collision leaves us stranded within the bounds of our own little selves. So when we are rejected and abandoned and left to ourselves as on a desert island without water or even a palm tree, our power turns out to be desperately constrained. The more you see yourself as abandoned and powerless, the more you wish for something or someone to come to the rescue. When the force that you yearn for corresponds to the image of something external, there's only one thing you wish to do: to offer it the submission of what little remains of you so as to mitigate the feeling that you are lacking all force. And as we all know, the relief is so intense that submission always brings a surge of joy.

Let's go back to the ghastly louts who trample on laws under your nose and put you, dear reader, in doubt about how to respond. What are you doing when you adopt the posture of a person who is in the right? It's perfectly clear, you are threatening them (justifiably, no argument) with the force of law, that is to say with the intervention of the state, whose role is to take your own words forward. There's an important point to mention here. By saying you are within your rights, you are doing nothing beyond making a threat – the threat of having the state intervene by force. The threat has an advantage: it turns the balance of power between you and the pillock into a conflict between said jerk and the big-machine-that's-tougher-than-you-are-you-stupid-oaf, and thus puts you theoretically under the protection of the authorities. Unfortunately, the threat also has a serious drawback: it puts the relationship onto a terrain where you have abandoned any attempt to work the forms of social interaction that could serve as levers for action; concretely, it puts you in a posture of submission (which might be justifiable, but that's not my point here). Once again, it is a posture you should use only in dire emergencies, just as you would jump off a moving train if and only if it was to escape certain death.

To sum up the direction of travel: when despicable idiots trample on laws that exist, the fact that you are the victim of their behaviour is so disturbing that you threaten them with the force of the state. In its turn, that act of submission to the powers that be weakens your own role as a social being, and therefore *increases* the likelihood of your being the victim of fools and knaves ... The vicious circle of submission closes around your neck. Rule-breakers and their incontinent four-legged friends can foul the whole road right in front of your eyes as you call down upon them the power of the state, which might even eventually come to your rescue ... but it also might not.

Might this lesson teach us to rely only on ourselves if we don't want to be slaves? Before I answer at greater length, please remember this:

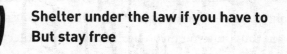

9   **Shelter under the law if you have to But stay free**

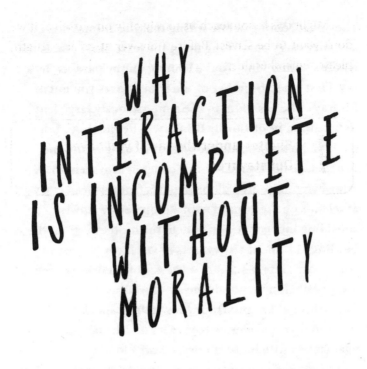

WHY
INTERACTION
IS INCOMPLETE
WITHOUT
MORALITY

They start coming in late spring making animal noises, and they carry on turning up in the least likely places the whole summer long. You're leaning on the parapet, let's say. First of all the father of the tribe shoves you out of his way so he has room to use a monstrously large lens to take what he obviously thinks will be the shot of the century. Meanwhile his brood are running round the promenade holding ice-cream cones at arm's length. A strawberry-flavoured globe departs from its trajectory and lands on the ground with a plop before slowly subsiding into goo. Upon which, the mother yells at the bawling kid, and their two sets of vocal cords create a soundscape reminiscent of a fire engine, a drill sergeant, a squad of Humvees and a posse of wailing mourners. You're brought round from your state of shock by a handful of inconsiderate teenagers who brush up against you with loose elbows, let off a loud fart, burst into guffaws, and run away to split their sides somewhere else.

The same identical scene can be experienced anywhere in the world, outside ancient palaces, in parks and gardens, on the steps of churches, outside mosques, sometimes even inside museums, until you can direct your steps on soles already tacky with chewing gum to wherever you can read a book in peace – anywhere out of this world.

In which we learn what moral authority is; and why you
have everything to lose if you try to use it on an idiot.

In the last chapter, we saw that when talking to boors and blockheads, reference to the law contains a more or less veiled threat, insofar as it alludes to a more or less tangible form of force. In this sense, the way we are able to threaten people who make our lives misery with at least the theoretical power of the state allows us to limit the damage dreadful idiots can do (concretely, by forestalling or punishing offences and crimes), but it also reassures us, for authority assuages our insufficiency when we have to deal with those slippery and variable beings we identify as damned fools. But I'm sorry to say there's a price to pay for the rule of law. The additional protection we *may* receive from the state (but which the state doesn't always provide) goes hand in hand with a reduction of autonomy. The more we feel sheltered, the less our reflexes of self-defence come into play. This effect would be called infantilisation if 'we' were only an individual. But what really needs protecting is not exactly our insignificant selves. What needs rescuing are our interactions. For instance, if you choose to carry a weapon, you might perhaps protect your physical self (and that's a big 'perhaps'), but you would instantly destroy what it would be worth protecting the self for –

namely, as I said, the quality of your interactions with others.

The third kind of case where you can say people are 'in the right' shows very pertinently how the person you are can actively accelerate the collapse of your interactions, at the precise point when you are trying to save them. Let's look at a case where you formulate a moral judgement about an action that is not prohibited by any written law – for example, being a jerk (and you can subsume under that term whatever action you want, such as lying, breaking a promise, fomenting disagreement, etc.). In such a case, you do not have facts on your side (as in cases of type 1) and you do not have the law on your side (as in cases of type 2). Moreover, you are not calling for an official ban on all jerks (as in type 1) or for applying an existing law that does ban jerks (type 2). So in heaven's name, what kind of 'right' are you talking about? Is there any moral rule forbidding people from being fuckwits?

Perhaps you are of the persuasion that somewhere out there you can find an intangible principle called *moral law*, which in this context simply means that it is *not written down*. Well, even if, like you, I feel I have some principles in my very bones, let us start by agreeing that moral law, because it commands and forbids, has the form of law, setting aside what gives it its actual reality: the *letter* (of the law) and the *force* (of institutions). So moral law is quite precisely the continuation of the law beyond its material framework, that is to say without written laws and without granting rewards and penalties. You could therefore think of moral authority as a pure and simple extrapolation of juridical law and dependent on a habit of submission; moreover, societies that have formed themselves into states are those where moralising discourse is the most developed. But let us take this step by step.

This first observation explains why saying and thinking you are *morally* in the right in ordinary life just means threatening idiots with a force that you do not possess and thus trying to establish a power relationship without having the means to do so. It's obviously stupid. You're behaving as if you were submitting yourself to the powers that be in a situation where there are none to be had.

Now, recall how submission works. As survivors (a description that seems more fitting than 'individuals') of an interactional crash become aware of their insufficiency, the more they wish for something to come to their rescue. When the state cannot respond to such an appeal (no state will ever make idiots illegal, seeing as they are in charge), such survivors offer their submission to a void, in other words to a *moral* authority, which this time round means an *absent* authority. Thanks to this image of a force in absentia, your own insufficiency in having your own position prevail is transformed into a demand. What you want without being able to get, you represent to yourself as a *moral right* that you have, that is to say as something that *belongs* to you even if you do *not* have it. What you expect from others without being able to oblige them to provide it, you represent to yourself as a moral duty incumbent on them, that is to say, something that they are *obliged* to do even when they do *not* do it. As you can now see, it's a kind of imaginative delirium, where reality is projected as a negative image of itself. It's similar to what shipwreck survivors on desert islands devoid of water and palm trees are doing when they dream of waterfalls and shade. So 'moral' now acquires a third meaning: it refers to what only occurs in a *theoretically ideal* space, which has no foundation other than the insufficient desire of stranded sailors, wallowing ever deeper in their insufficiency, flailing around for the force they no longer have. For example, you, my dear reader, maintain that human beings have a *duty* not to be jerks. What's more, you have the cheek to think that you are not supposed to hate your fellow humans even if they are jerks. Well, well! Duties of that calibre do no honour to your sense of reality, none at all …

But they do you honour all the same. Here's why.

On the one hand, we can say that the *moral authority* you assert expresses a differential between your wishes and the real world. Consequently, this authority does not derive from a positive absolute loudly issuing its decrees; but it does express an authentic absolute – the stranded sailor's Great Appeal, the Great Challenge that the lost sailor confronts you with. It is the voice of your insufficiency, it is your personal demand to fill the gap between what you wish for and the events that occur. At this level of analysis, it is possible that the most suitable form of expression for people suffering from the utter mess that stupidity and boorishness make of our lives – the living spring of all morality under the sun – is purely and simply a cry of anguish, or an exorcising dance, or whatever else that allows you to overcome what I previously dubbed the lamenting of trust, in other words, the terrifying emotions caused by the collapse of human interaction. Of course it is! For as I have already shown, that catastrophic crash puts all human rules in a state of crisis, so that when you feel you are in such a situation of distress or insufficiency, you are entirely free to express your dismay in any way you like. You have only yourself to rely on when faced with the fundamental poetic problem – how to spill out your emotion to the last drop.

This is where the moral system can be saved from absurdity. In the last analysis, the main function of the division between Good and Evil is to justify your moaning, and to authorise your wailing, alongside strengthening your effort when you are in despair. Yes indeed! If your beloved cheats on you, lies to you, manipulates you and leads you by the nose into the muddy terrain of cowardice, or when your partner mistreats you or hits you, the moment you say 'This is bad, I will never put up with it', it feels like a liberation. Helping you to break up, helping you to act, helping you maintain a *theoretically ideal* image of yourself – those are the great virtues of morality, and its positive role. And it is not nothing: the break frees up your emotions, releases you from your misplaced submission. That usually lets off a huge cloud of emotions containing, among other things, a lot of relief and a great deal of pain. Your accusations, judgements and sentences in the several imaginary trials that you conduct, and which allow you to invent atrocious punishments for the person you put in the dock, have the merit of making the cloud dissipate – it will rain hot ashes or heart-sinking grey drizzle, as the case may be. In this sense, morality is a directly affective device. Its cut-and-dried formulas turn out to be able to receive, absorb and express what we feel.

However, moral law also has a destructive function that it performs perfectly well – even a little *too* well. In fact, morality destroys interaction, which is very helpful in harmful interactions, as I have just shown. But its great drawback is that it destroys *all* interactions – as you can easily see when you argue with your friends about questions that call for a moral response. Who knows what to do about your ex? Did your partner really cheat on you? From what date and for which action does that louse deserve to be treated as a dickhead? By whom? Once questions like these are on the table, the tone rises, the tension increases, and at some point – a foreseeable one, if you're paying attention – the discussion breaks down. Why is that? Because moral law is a way of talking and thinking immediately proximate to individual insufficiency. And that, by the way, is why gossip is so fascinating: it makes a spectacle of the insufficiency of other people. This is rather comforting, since it proves we are not the only crash survivors on the planet. But the main thing is that this is the foundation of moral law. Its authority comes from your own situation as the survivor of a catastrophe, and it certainly does authorise you to formulate an absolute imperative: to survive. However, as you surely grasp, this absolute is valid only for you, since you are the Lone Survivor from the capsized liner you were on. That is also why, when we talk about moral rights, we always get excited about something that we ought to have agreed on before starting to talk about it. So the discussion becomes an untidy way for each participant to require silent agreement from the others for prior consent to the discussion itself, or maybe a scream of terror that would bring them together like a pack of wolves howling fearfully in the misty dark.

That is how insufficiency and what it calls for end up turning the natural order of things on its head. In fact, we can establish the conditions for our relationships (that is to say, rules of morality) only on the basis of a negotiation *between* us. To set conditions for a dialogue is therefore a contradiction in terms: a dialogue can have no preconditions. That is why it is necessary to lay down your arms whenever these subjects are raised: our moral convictions are immediately proximate to our insufficiency. We end up tearing each other to shreds because each of us tries to silently repress the emotion that he or she feels in the face of his or her individual insufficiency. It's a noble aim, but a lousy method. To put it in philosophical terms, speech is an unconditional, because it is by nature conditioning.

In sum, it's better to recognise the general insufficiency of other people from the get-go, so as to start on the right foot, which is to admit that we will only get over insufficiency and anguish by improvising a form of open normativity through speech, in conversation with others. That can't rely on moral authority, because moral authority can only be grounded in each individual: it relies on the relationship between your attempt to survive and your awareness of your inability to achieve it on your own. Once moral authority is involved in an interaction with another person, group or institution, the anguish that you invest in your personal moral code perverts the relationship, because it contains a hidden threat by means of which your moral code claims to set conditions. Its motto is: *We have to talk about that – or else!*

Or else … what? I'll get on to that in a minute. For the moment, I want to exit from this area of conceptual turbulence, which has worn you out (and me too), by concluding on this point. Moral law seeks application without conditions, and that means, by force – knowing that it has no force, except the ability to get on everybody's nerves by irritating and exacerbating their anguish. That is why standing on morality is a sure-fire way of putting your relationships to the axe.

Does that make me an immoralist? No. I am just making explicit a criterion that you already respect when you talk with your nearest and dearest. You avoid getting angry unnecessarily, that is to say, you respect the privilege of interaction over the content of the exchange. That really does not mean you give up on your moral principles, because to my mind it is only natural that norms be normative (including most especially those that seem utterly obvious, such as love, sincerity and good will). On the other hand, don't try to apply your personal moral norms in conditions that are in direct contradiction to them. Trying to impose them by force is to betray them. Think about this: to impose your own norms is the surest way of wrecking whatever part of them might be shared with others.

10 **Don't impose your own norms**
Negotiate the norms of others

WHY IDIOTS LIKE DESTRUCTION

Who's the Idiot?

'Can I have fries on the side?'

'The lunch menu comes with a salad and green beans.'

'But I know you've got fries. Look, there they are, on the à la carte menu.'

'But you haven't ordered à la carte.'

'Well, what if I pay extra? One pound? Two?'

'If you want to order à la carte, I can certainly bring fries on the side.'

'But that costs twice as much! No way!'

'In that case, I'll bring you the dish of the day with a salad and green beans.'

In which we discern a strategy for surviving family meals by contemplating the balance of power and the art of war.

When I woke up this morning, it occurred to me that the last sentence of the previous chapter could give rise to a serious objection. I wrote: to impose your own norms is the surest way of wrecking whatever part of them might be shared with others. The sentence hadn't come to me just like that, in a burst of inspiration. It had taken me fifteen years of learning, teaching and living in the four corners of the world. What, just for that sentence? I hear you say. However, just as I was wondering where to have the sentence tattooed on my body, a doubt crept into my mind: whether my accepting the existence of normative tendencies (which explains why we believe, justifiably, that idiots exist) while simultaneously rejecting their forcible application (which means that we *cannot* destroy idiots, even at the level of a moral ideal) didn't make me an advocate of a subtle kind of manipulation. Was I not advising you to avoid confronting jerks and idiots but to manipulate them (which runs the risk of allowing them to smother you in turn), provided you do it *gently*?

Well, here's my answer. When I said your norms were shareable, I meant to encourage you to engage in negotiations on the basis of shared and reciprocal rights and powers. There is no reason for any such ethics of interaction to be seen as a veiled form of domination. We can imagine the outcome of the dialogue being a modification of norms, making them susceptible to perhaps infinite variation. If you then say that this variation would cause them to cease to be norms, well then, you've understood my point. Without ruffling the conviction that everybody *ought* to share your value system, you can now nonetheless neutralise the negative effects of this tendency. To put it another way, you can remain faithful to yourself and yet still give up being the idiot of someone else. It's already quite enough of a burden to have an idiot of your own.

Moreover, imagine the opposite hypothesis. We got to glimpse it when we examined preaching, the principles of law, and moral authority: outside negotiation, there is only a balance of force, and here, *force* is not metaphorical. If you can please keep in mind that violence is never more than a hair's breadth away, we can now propose a new part of our definition: in principle and by definition, *idiots are always pro-war*.

Yes, I know, if you say *I'm in favour of peace*, then you'll have all your interlocutors on your side and especially the biggest idiots among them. However, the reality is that many of our postures in daily life are oriented towards conflict and destruction, though we don't realise it. In fact, whenever we set prior conditions for dialogue – conditions that presuppose the other is not in fact other – stupidity winkles its way in without even noticing, so to speak. The idea that the other must *first* be destroyed so as to *then* have the right to speak is a stupid posture, but one that is more widespread than you might think.

Although it's not my custom to do this, I'm going to illustrate my point with the saying of a great man, whose image has been in the back of my mind since the beginning of this investigation. Cato the Younger was haunted by the thought of his enemies. After the Second Punic War between Rome and Carthage, the great senator, a hero of Roman history, always ended his speeches with the same sentence. After giving his speech in the Senate, irrespective of the subject of the debate, Cato would always go back to his seat saying: *Ceterum censeo Carthaginem esse delendam*, 'However, I think Carthage should be destroyed.'

Cato's obsession with destroying his enemies – and the fact that we still remember him and his ultimately monstrous saying two thousand years on – should remind us that the logic of war continues to smoulder like red-hot lava beneath the outer crust of any debate. Unfortunately, and unlike Cato, idiots do not realise that we have no third alternative: either we agree to get on with each other, or else we silently acquiesce in the fact that, all in all, it would be better if we just slaughtered each other. With an ingenuity that takes us by surprise every time, idiots are almost permanently in favour of war. They forget that in the wake of words real conflicts arise and that in 146 BCE, Carthage was razed to the ground. Cato had long been dead.

What connection can there be between a sister-in-law one sandwich short of the full picnic or a motormouth taxi driver who drones on about Islam, Judeo-Christian civilisation, Mamils, fascists and professors, and tragic bombing raids taking place not so far away? We have to agree that the connection is a very loose and distant one – but it is real nonetheless. We're obviously not dealing with cause and effect here, even less with moral responsibility. The issue is the logic of war. Idiots want war without having any idea what it is, or any real desire to wage it. But the principle of war, in the form of depriving another person of the right to speak (and fundamentally, of the right to exist), provides them with what someone claiming to be 'in the right' can only express indirectly: the pleasure (most often symbolic, implicit and vague) of exercising the power to destroy.

That is why idiots and jerks draw a paradoxical pleasure from favouring war. They get a kick out of destruction, at least in theory, and that kick is a danger to us all, in principle and in reality. Are you perhaps wondering where their special pleasure in destruction comes from? Well, to begin with, blockheads and boors are nothing more than pea-brained giants who can't get over how strong they are, and they remain astounded by their strength even as they use it. Like newborn infants, they want to test their power against anything within their reach, at any cost – particularly as their power remains problematic for them. With their own doubts amplified by other idiots who dominate them, they never cease to doubt themselves. Some assuage their anxieties principally by asserting themselves, others by submitting. However, within the span of a single day, their polymorphous idiocy oscillates between one form and another – from domination to submission to destruction.

But there is much more to this. When jerks and dick-heads incline towards destruction (for example, when they make threats) they don't care whether the force they call on is theirs or not. Indeed, very often, they don't care whether it protects them themselves. So what do they care about? Well, they are blindly obedient to a logic of the economy of forces, which is not particular to them, because it is a natural tendency of the universe. It is simpler and easier to destroy than to build, to attack than to pacify, to wreck than to understand. Idiots channel a form of violence that goes far beyond the confines of any subjectivity, social construction, political compact or ecology. In other words, they respect nature's law of entropy – the return to disorder or destruction of organised forms – not exactly because they are lazy (though it is not wrong to say that they are), but more deeply because the force they channel fails to become organised in them, fails to complete itself as subjectivity, and therefore collapses on the shore of relationships like a beached whale.

The preference for war that can be found in idiots is therefore not the sign of some mysterious death wish. The violence they call on and that they embody is not only a form of power that a person may exercise on and against another. The violence of jerks and oafs is more *cosmic* than that. It represents the fact that humans are channels for a force that may unite or split asunder, cohere or make incoherent, and that can crush humans alongside the whole planet Earth more easily than you can blow the fluff off a dandelion. What causes true destruction (war, deaths, ecological catastrophes) is therefore nothing other than the sublime force of being which sometimes structures itself in wonderful combinations of energy – in you, in life, in joy, in the eternal spring of the universe – and sometimes collapses in terrifying bursts that reveal the great fragility and rarity of the phenomena that allow subjects to organise themselves and define their own points of view in the world. I hear you! You would like idiots to suffer and to weep, to give you their hand, to smile and look quaint. But they won't. The force of existence passes through them and destroys them, and for that reason they suffer and hate. And they will hate pretty much anything and anybody because the force they channel is a destructive one.

Being more immediate, more simple and less costly in short-term resources than dialogue, destruction is ultimately consubstantial with stupidity. At this stage, almost all of this philosophical inquiry thus finds itself obliged to go into reverse. For as you can now see, it is not possible for stupidity to be destroyed, *because stupidity is the principle of all destruction*. That's why the biggest idiots are sacred cows for philosophers, who know that in any case they cannot make themselves understood and for that reason they strictly refrain from trying. Is this philosophical posture – too often mistaken for aristocratic disdain – not itself in the end pretentious and scornful? Be careful how you take that objection: a posture opposite to the silence of philosophers with respect to fools would immediately unleash the logic of war; contrary to appearances, it would not be called respect, but intolerance. Leave the idiots be, and let them chew the cud of their wars; sometimes, that is the only way to let sacred cows graze in peace.

So if you want to be as far as possible in the camp of the good and the smart, you should never fail to let idiots say what they have to say. To put it more precisely, you should leave your nearest and dearest entirely free to spout utter rubbish. For if you seriously seek to persuade them (*except in the form of play*), you would put yourself on the dark side straight away. So it really doesn't matter if you have truth, reason or whatever to back you up, you would just be another idiot throwing your anguish at others like a custard pie. Especially when at a family dinner, where all that matters is the bond that brings (or tries to bring) relatives together, you should learn to appreciate the utterances of the miraculous cattle instead of letting them get on your nerves. Always pay attention to what they are saying, so as to relieve them of their complaints, and do not fail to see in them the god Shiva, who in his dance of a thousand arms destroys the world with a smile. For idiots, my dear friends, are the holy apostles of war. War is not just a scandal. What is horrifying about war is that it reveals like a black hole the ecstatic implosion of joy without cause.

11 Make peace
And leave idiots to their wars

WHY WE ARE RULED BY IDIOTS

Anyone who has enjoyed watching a colony of seals bask in the sun must have realised that stupidity, like intelligence, is not a uniquely human feature. There's no lack of room on the vast rocky shore, but troublemakers are not in short supply. They prefer already occupied spots to available lounging areas. So they start pointless fights, prompting squeals and injuries. They make the lives of the others miserable in every way they can – by taking dives that send splashes all over the place, by trying to get seals that are bigger than they are to give up their places, and also sometimes attacking smaller ones. That's the drama of all communities. Where there is interaction, there are jerks.

In which we acknowledge the legitimacy of idiots within social hierarchies, even and especially when they rank higher than you. Which does not prevent fights from breaking out.

It is very difficult to disregard the stupidity of other people so as to hear the suffering they express. When the idiot is your boss, it becomes virtually unachievable. My heart bleeds for you, my dear readers, when I see you professionally obliged to apply crazy decisions made by idiots higher up the chain, or to carry out counter-productive actions, or to have your work trashed by someone else. It's one thing to allow human bloody-mindedness to give you a glimpse of the power of the universe; quite another to let it wrestle you to the ground, block possibilities, wear down good will, commit injustice, mess up the world and require you to join in …

I'm not talking about aesthetics, morality, law or metaphysics here. The issue here is a scandal that you would think anyone would acknowledge out of basic common sense, especially as it has major economic, political and philosophical consequences. I am talking about the madness of giving public office to intellectually challenged, twisted and brazen idiots, and the horror that ensues of our having to get along with them.

Let's leave the last point to one side. You'll agree that the presence of this piece of human shit in that job offends you, because unlike the cosmic dance of Shiva, it connects your own position directly to disorder and chaos. You therefore reckon quite naturally that things are not as they should be, that such a skunk should on no account have been given a job where all it does is wreck the prospects of all and sundry. If you permit, we will therefore co-author a revision of that line of code in the program of the universe, so as to make your irritation justifiable: namely, to say that the world would be a better place if it were run by competent folk. Over the next few pages, I will show you that it would not.

In this field, it is really necessary to avoid empty generalities, so I will focus on what I know best, university research and teaching, and hopefully others will be able to apply the lessons to their own environment. As you can imagine, there are quite a number of undistinguished minds among professional philosophers. Those who make real advances in the field are vastly outnumbered by second-rate cooks who warm up old dishes or regurgitate them. The majority of them publish depressingly banal papers that don't take anything a step forward. But what would happen if we took this complaint seriously and satisfied the wish it expresses? We would have to cut down the number of philosophy professors so only the very best remained in post. Leaving aside the tricky question of how to select them, that would leave just a few hundred professional philosophers in the world. This tiny elite would then be completely isolated, lacking professors misrepresenting their work, lacking amateur readers who fail to understand their articles. So what would happen then? A crisis would arise from the wishes of members of this elite to communicate with each other. Because they would have lost all external input, they would recreate a division among themselves so as to separate the wheat from the chaff, and in a sense, they would reinvent new forms of stupidity. As there would be several iterations of such an operation, members of the elite would end up losing their taste for each other's company.

This brief mind game (which is being played in earnest in some countries already) brings out the fact that any social agent (scholar, professor, or whatever else) only exists in a context of support, and inside a whole society that not only makes such activities relevant, but also funds them. As a result, you have to admit that the *naturally* elitist tendency of people of quality, who typically prefer each other's company and select themselves as the only legitimate holders of power, runs the risk of destroying the elite itself when preference becomes exclusion. I'm not yet proposing to put idiots in charge of the elite, but please be patient.

The first leg of my reasoning sought to show not only that asking for excellence is evidence of a tendency to associate merit (competence in a given field) with the power to make decisions that serve the interests of the given field or undertaking; but also, that you cannot entirely exclude mediocre and incompetent actors without the risk of thinning the field until it is close to bare. At this stage, you will surely grant that idiots are necessary, if only in subaltern positions. You will also agree that an elite based on merit can only exist through the assent and participation of a larger body of people whose efforts enable and validate the intelligence, competence, efficiency and so forth of the smaller group. I'm not dealing here with the fact that the meritocratic ideal justifies inequality, in virtue of the fact that it has the reciprocal implication that the privileged should at least theoretically deserve their status, and that those who do not have such privileges don't deserve to have them (something that the wisdom of the ages has been strenuously denying for the last three thousand years – in vain, since the subordinated classes will always refuse to deny submission to the dominant classes, for as you know, they draw pleasure from it). I want only to insist on one point: without second-rate people, the first-rate folk would not exist as such, and could not even *wish* for what they wish for.

Now we move to the second stage of the argument. For you must allow that there is a *community of desire* uniting the one and the other. The boundary between competence and incompetence doesn't prevent people who think they are better and those they consider idiots from being in the same boat. It is possible that idiots are unaware of the community; but that would mean that they are only accidental obstacles to the common good, and that they are opposed to it opportunistically, by chance, as circumstances permit. Willy-nilly, and whether they know it or not, idiots are part of a system of desire (what is called a society), without which we would not even know what to want.

Now comes the great leap. Even if you are a benighted royalist, or believe that ships' captains rule over their crews by the radiant grace of their own virtues, you have to admit that nothing human can stay afloat in this world – kingship, galley-slaving, aircraft carriers – without majority support. And the excellence of the Romantic genius, a Greek hero, or the self-made man would have no meaning without the power to attract and retain the desire of the lowing herd that initially failed to recognise them. Admittedly, you want to maintain that genius is a mystery, or a gift of God. But I don't need to reject this point to state that if outstanding geniuses are not to pass through this world without ever being noticed, they have to interact with a shared desire so that their glorification can nonetheless take place among mere mortals. As a result, you must allow that a community of desire plays at least an equal part to that of the genius. Nobody is the perfect embodiment of that common desire, but it is that desire which determines the social ranks that all of us occupy by virtue of our individual manner of negotiating with it. (Including, by the way, when we lose out in the negotiation.)

In such conditions, power positions have to be entrusted to people who wish for them; and the people who wish for them are necessarily those who are most adept at exploiting institutional nooks and crannies, most inclined to flatter others and be humiliated by them, and most able to embody (partly by misapprehension) the hazy 'will of the greatest number'. But that doesn't imply the truth of the misanthropic saying that most people are idiots; rather, it derives from the great diversity of human beings, such that it is very difficult to establish an average or a typical individual, or anything that gives adequate expression to our problematic unity. (In this connection you might like to note that no *average persons* exist in any community, because they would have one testicle and one breast each.)

And this is where idiots are victorious. Their personal mediocrity makes it easier for them to slip into the costume of the average person and to give that theoretical person a face. That's why the natural condition of society is not strictly speaking the reign of mediocrity (which you could call mediocracy if you looked at it from the point of view of a 'superior') but *medianocracy* – in other words, the fact that an ungraspable median ends up being embodied by mediocracy. With the effect that power will most probably but not inevitably fall into the hands of some idiot or other.

Now you understand why having an idiot for your boss or your prime minister is not a matter of bad luck or injustice or even a surprise, since it is the result of the law of probability. This observation ought to help you keep one of the most difficult balancing acts there is, between your striving for a better world (which involves struggling against idiots and preventing them from doing harm, always and only within your capacities) and your understanding of the world, which by assuaging your feelings helps you not to experience stupid decisions as cosmic disturbances. In other terms, change the world not because it disgusts you, but because you love it – including the way it currently is. That doesn't stop you from having your own preferences.

To reach that state of balance, remember two things. First, that each of us is more or less where he or she should be in this world, and it is *for that reason* and *not despite that reason* that idiots are in charge in politics and business and more or less everywhere else. Second, that if you think you are not in your rightful place, then that may *possibly* be an injustice, but it is *without doubt* the challenge you have to meet.

**12 Fight for your preferences
Not for your frustrations**

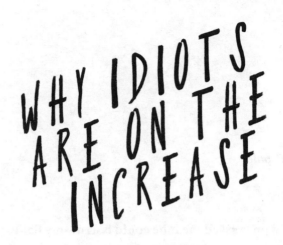

WHY IDIOTS ARE ON THE INCREASE

Party People

A friend once asked me if he could borrow my flat to throw a party. I said OK, but please let me know when you want it. One evening he just turned up, and didn't even apologise for not having called in advance. A gaggle of friends loitered in the street outside. In alarm, I asked how many people he'd invited, and how late they would stay. Not to worry, he said, there's thirty or so still to come, but I'll have a nap on your sofa before it really begins. Then he started telling his mates where to put the case of vodka and where to plug in the sound system. Why don't you stay and join in the fun? he asked. Or are you still writing that old book about philosophy? Yes, I am, I replied – but actually, no, I'm going to start on a different book right now.

*In which we learn how to overcome the infernal growth
in the number of idiots, and make acquaintance with the
author's grandmother, Mme Yvette Gibertaud.*

I've taken refuge in my bedroom, my dear unhappy friends, and I appeal to you to come and face one of the greatest mysteries of human life with me. How is it possible for the number of idiots and boors to be forever on the increase? Where do they all come from? Why, oh why are there so many of them?

A moment's thought makes this observation seem like an optical illusion. After all, why should there be more twits and scoundrels today than yesterday? However, you must remember that an idiot is an event that occurs within a human relationship, not a type of human being walking around in the street: that is what you could call the interactional nature of idiocy. And it is not exactly news to say that the number of our interactions is on the increase. Our forebears, broadly speaking, lived in societies that were less mobile, and so most of them encountered fewer unfamiliar people in the course of their lives. Even our parents travelled long distances less frequently than we do, did not meet as many people as we do, and because of generally more linear lines of travel, they surely did not frequent as many different social environments as we do. Lastly, internet platforms and phone apps have hugely expanded the potential for establishing contact with people near and far, through text and image, one-to-one or in shared spaces. Obviously, the more interactions there are, the more opportunities arise for misunderstanding, for clumsiness or, in brief, for interactional disasters. So instead of having to cope in the course of your life with a few dozen boneheads of the first order (according to my grandmother, a dozen of them could be unambiguously located on a line going from her own village to the next), you now have to come up against several hundred. And so my first conclusion is that increasing rates of interaction cause a rise in the number of idiots. Q.E.D.

You might nonetheless want to point out that as the number of idiots increases, each has a proportionately less serious impact on our lives. Indeed, my grandmother could not easily sidestep the major nutcases in her path; whereas most of the jerks you and I come across nowadays remain pretty much unknown – even leaving aside the virtual boors we encounter in cyberspace. So it is not absurd to claim that although there are more idiots around, they spend a lot less time in our lives. That is my second conclusion.

Sad to say, part of this benefit is lost, because our own patience and tolerance have also decreased in proportion. My grandmother had to decide on her preferences among the actual people of her own village and its surrounding area; over time, she could see how their characters evolved, and with hope against hope she could modify and improve her relationships, even with her mother-in-law (but let's not go too far, because some people are *really* hardcore idiots). On the other hand, when you have to cope with a theoretically unlimited number of interlocutors, there's no fence or prop to force or help you to make a moral adaptation, and you'll no doubt tell me, blending realism with bad faith, that you haven't got time anyway (because the only injunctions you acknowledge are professional, not philosophical ones, and more's the pity). As a result, you simply rule out of account people whose personal flaws and blemishes could perhaps be coped with, and who are in any case susceptible to change over time. You've turned into high-precision machines capable of spotting idiots by the blink in their eye. You've become merciless graders of people into idiots and others, to ensure that nobody gets in your way. So I come to a third conclusion: idiots are ever more numerous because you have become more sensitive to them than ever before. Q.E.D.

However, this last observation brings out the complex interplay of preferences that allows each of us to assert ourselves as human beings. If I may sum up two centuries of sociology in a single sentence, we become ourselves by mastering codes which allow individuals to assert themselves as members of various groups, while also meeting their need to assert their difference, which is experienced in different ways in different groups (which implies interacting more or less willingly with the norms of that group).

What's happening today is a gigantic mixing and blending of group norms. Different ways of speaking (including speaking different languages), different ways of dressing and laughing, walking and sitting, different ways of interpreting events, of feeling and expressing emotion, of imagining time and space, the self and the other – in sum, all the variations of what is called human sensibility are being mixed up and brought together in places (especially major cities) where people feel themselves to be more diverse than ever before. Today's cosmopolitanism thus fosters the fracturing of social codes into micro-communities; idiots constitute a sub-group within each of them. As we know, idiots can be spotted for rejecting people who do not follow their codes, and on this point idiocy is evenly distributed among the dominant and the dominated, left and right, rich and poor, irrespective of the privileges afforded or denied them, among the learned and the uneducated, atheists and believers, men and women, and so on, since stupidity, in this context, does not imply adherence to any group, only the way that adherence is performed, by making exclusion a preferred means of action. That's how differences that were formerly conceived of as differences of civilisation, race, gender or culture decline in proportion to their renaissance in the form of less homogenous societies. Once again my conclusion is: because codes are being whittled away, idiots are on the increase. Q.E.D.

In such circumstances, as argued above, the crumbling of codes is in part offset by the fact that differences between human communities have become ever less spectacular. The most sensitive of them (language, dress, etc.) are trending towards global uniformity, and so you might expect phenomena of rejection to decline as well, as differences melt away. But as I also argued above (see the second demonstration), standardisation is in turn offset by the fact that irritability (or let's say, the weakening of people's patience in the face of perceptible differences) increases proportionately.

So let us stop to think for a moment. As algorithms become more efficient and as they are ever more widely used, our societies tend towards the personalisation of goods and services, making them ever better-targeted to you, dear John or dear Jane ... As a result, codes of inclusion and exclusion, with increasing intensity and precision, come ever closer to actual individuals. Do you see what I am getting at? Ensconced in ever more personalised codes based on ever tinier details, each of you will soon become (at least in theory) the *only* person respecting those codes as they appear to you (at least on your screen). That's how idiots will have succeeded in multiplying so much that you will seem in your own eyes to be the *last human being left on Earth* – alongside maybe a handful of friends – in a vast ocean of twits and oafs.

In such a situation, there's no point promoting the benefits of tolerance by claiming that we must accept each other as different so as to be part of the same happy circle. Collaborative moralism of that kind is absurd. To be different is, precisely, to have preferences, which include a natural tendency towards repulsion. So it is just as pointless to reject repulsion as it is to lament submission, since idiots, by definition, will never agree to join your jolly conga.

How do we get out of this? Well, let's look at it the other way round. Even granted that our society has known times of greater sameness, do you seriously maintain that observance of a single set of spelling rules, or adherence to a single set of grammar rules, or to a lexicon with no variants, or privileging a whiter kind of skin or a better-powdered wig proved that folk were smarter in the old days? And what crazy nostalgic musing would lead you to think that shrinking the number of human relationships would allow us to recover a serenity that even my grandmother (who is definitely not a bore) never really experienced? Anyway, speaking for a moment as a historian, are you really sure that the supposed uniformity of codes in past ages is not a retrospective illusion, created by the selectivity of the sources that we have? You may say that my examples are superficial, and that the least stupid people know full well that external appearances do not matter. For instance, they know that under the miniskirts and hijabs worn by women what matters is the freedom to choose. But apart from the fact that idiots are precisely the people who do not know this, my attack bears on a way of conceiving freedom as a choice between two superficial and perfectly insignificant choices.

Yes, indeed! If you want to stem the irresistible rising tide of idiots before you join it as idiot number one, you must grant that the transformation of dress codes (and thus of the *very forms of freedom*) into *moral values* is exactly what moves us to transform repulsion into exclusion, so that in the end you see idiots everywhere. By inserting the hallowed notion of values into trivial everyday issues, you infringe the precept given to us by our greatest sages to stop making judgements about our fellow humans all the time.

I see you are hesitating ... Are we not supposed to defend our own values? I answer: if you really care about your values, above all else do not *defend* them! Waving them about like crusader banners is not the way to spread them or to defeat stupidity. Because what distinguishes you from twits and oafs are not the values you hold, as I do not tire of repeating, but the way you relate to other people and the quality of such relationships. Insofar as they express your attachment to certain kinds of relationships, your values have all my sympathy. But they are doomed to be counter-productive in proportion to the degree to which you assert them to be unconditional. Freedom, for instance, is never unconditional – it refers to the ability to plough your own furrow in existing circumstances, that is to say under precise and specific conditions.

So when you think about it, the fact of having values is *not* what distinguishes one set of people from another – thank goodness! – and the idea that our values set us apart is itself idiotic, since it attributes a local specificity to what is intended in its own terms to overcome divisions and not to justify them. So you can't say, for instance, that *your* ideal is freedom while not denying other people the right to see it as their own. I can't think of anything more dangerous than that, since you would be making an enemy out of anyone who conceives of freedom in a different way from you.

So please admit that, instead of defending values, you would do better to develop relationships, in other words, to seek to reduce the extent and the number of mis-understandings. Because as you may recall, misunder-standing is the main source of the growth in the number of idiots. So you can't inhibit their increase by going back to the colonial universalism of the French Enlightenment, or by the person-centred relativism of the digital era. The only way to do it is by breaking free from your defensive posture, putting your ideal values to the test of concrete interactions and engaging in negotiation so as to improve your relationships on all fronts, for that will weaken idiots among all groups. To put it another way: make improvements to the house that is yours, instead of judgements about the houses of others.

> ## 13 Look after your interactions
> ## Your values will look after themselves

WHY IDIOTS
ALWAYS WIN

Stupidity is one of the attributes that human beings always want to assign to their own kind; but even on that point they are on the wrong track.

It's easy to test this out. A pebble in your shoe doesn't need to be endowed with intentionality to piss you off.

In which a method will be proposed for interacting with knaves and fools, based on a specific conception of their world, your world and your respective personalities.

It's possible you got the impression that the last chapter treated stupidity as a mere phenomenon of representation, as if it were just an illusion. Maybe you are hoping you're well on the way to a conclusion where, in a state of purely philosophical ecstasy, you and I will overcome stupidity together and see reconciliation spread over the world at long last. Allow me to adjust the focus. On the one hand, I do indeed maintain that the impression that idiots are on the increase, whether or not that impression fits real historical determinations, will never stop, even if in actual fact the number of idiots goes down. Why so? The real reason is that idiots do not increase in terms of any historical chronology. As we grow older, the number of idiots rises in proportion to our progressive loss of illusions about the unity of the human phenomenon and the possibility of sharing our own norms with others. So as the idiot in you starts to wilt, thousands of others rise up from the ground like weeds on the lawn. In that sense, we can say that idiots increase in direct proportion to our ceasing to be such.

However, losing our naivety doesn't stop our brains from finding other balls to chain to our ankles. As your life experience grows longer, so, in successive steps, social change, urban renewal and technological advance destroy the framework of your memories. When you look at the current state of the street where you grew up, when you learn (from hearsay, of course) about how young people hook up and copulate nowadays, and so forth, you are overcome with nostalgia. I know how you feel, dear reader! Individual nostalgia, created by the strangeness of the new, can't be denied or repressed without endangering our entire society, for it reveals a fundamental principle which demonstrates the main force of idiots, which is inertia.

What is the source of this inertia – the kind you can guess lies behind *fixed ideas*, *narrow minds*, and the like? To understand it we have to begin with its opposite, adaptation. Adaptation is the product of a relatively long learning curve, starting with the privileged period of childhood, that supplies information that is imprinted on the least conscious levels of our being. It draws on a whole range of experiences that includes the space where you live, the nature of the sense impressions you most commonly have (sound, touch, and so on) and the interactions you have with other people (the language they speak, etc.) – in sum, everything that makes up what each of us calls the 'real world'. Replicating some kinds of behaviour automatically, associating particular ideas, or valuing specific forms of speech depends directly on the 'real world' to which these behaviours and representations refer. In fact, people adopt or refine almost everything that defines them as individuals on the basis of the imperative of adaptation. It comes to what I shall now call a 'personality', in the sense of a singular disposition (that is neither entirely predictable nor entirely arbitrary) to react to events in a particular way. It's a notion that incorporates so many social, genetic and symbolic determinants, alongside conscious and unconscious experiences laid down over time in complex and confusing ways, that nobody yet knows how to disentangle them from it.

Well, then: putting aside the question of where our personalities ultimately come from, we can say that the real world of experience is a major factor of constraint. As a result, human beings do not change their opinions, perspectives or behaviour unless they are constrained to modify their reference worlds by new experiences. Only updates to their 'real worlds' allow people to adjust their personalities: it's quite impossible to change yourself just by saying so. (That is crushingly obvious, and I reckon everybody knows it to be true, even if only to forgive themselves for their own flaws. Pop-culture nostrums about the efficacy of 'willpower' are just ridiculous.) In short, if you inhabit a 'world' where a well-ordered argument is treated as a relevant contribution, then my reasoning may be enough to win you over. But if that is not the case, then an image might do the trick better, or else a video clip or an emoji or whatever else you treat as relevant contributions to your relationship to the real world.

Unfortunately, it is not so easy to change your reference world. A peculiar feedback loop means that a personality tends to defend the world to which it has first adapted. Thus comes into being a circle uniting the self and the world, such that you cannot change the personality without changing its world; reciprocally, moreover, the personality's force of inertia protects its world from change. To put it in *their* words: an attack on the one is an attack on the other.

Consequently, you can't change the representations of idiots unless you take account of the fact that their idiocy is in the first place the result of adaptation. In the last analysis, their inertia or blinkered state is the result of more or less successful adaptations to specific factors, however obsolete, mistaken or partial they may be. You need a lot of tact to change them (their opinions, behaviours, etc.) and you need to take advantage of the gaps and breaches in their reference worlds with the greatest delicacy and stop short of overturning their personalities. It's a judgement call every time, there's no all-purpose recipe, except that struggling against the inertia of idiots implies overall that you are seeking to enlighten them about changes that have *already occurred* in their 'real worlds' and can show them how necessary it is to take those changes into account in a way that is relevant to them – and you should use a cartoon or an advertising jingle to do that in preference to giving a demonstration in words.

But while you already feel prepared to teach lessons, please remember that the dynamic of integrating new elements into a 'real world' is reciprocal by definition. That means that the way the shithead or harridan you're talking to integrates what you are saying to them depends in strict proportion on your capacity to take into account the mental worlds of idiots; you have to accept (if only on grounds of their existing) that they are *de facto* one part of the truth. Thus you cannot be certain that your own mental world is not entirely idiotic unless you – you in the first place – are able to acknowledge the reality of that world for which idiots are the evidence. For that world is the very proof of a gap or fissure in your own.

Overcoming stupidity thus necessarily implies modifying two worlds by reciprocal elision, grounded in the presence of fissures in both of them. Don't worry, changing worlds is not just your responsibility alone. Taking the long view, you can leave History to change them by itself quite naturally; whatever 'conservatives' may say, History doesn't just make itself. And it never goes into reverse. We have no choice but to participate in changes already under way by striving to *steer* historical evolution towards preferences that we must constantly revise and update.

Now we are at a crux. We're playing for our future (or what we imagine as our future) and we must either win or lose. Hey ho! We are going to lose almost every match against boors and boneheads – but not quite every one. Why? Not because idiots are in the majority – that would be absurd. Since idiots are interactional entities, idiots simply *cannot* be tallied! On the other hand it is correct to say that the majority of people are necessarily stupid, since most human beings tend to follow the principle of the conservation of energy. That's it. Nothing else. Just laziness, carelessness, incompetence and conformism. In the end all these terms come down to the same thing, to the good old principle of inertia. In this sense, idiots almost always win, thanks to Nature's natural bent. You and I keep up the struggle to change things step by step, and to prompt our societies to adapt in constructive and subtle ways that have a low probability of taking place. But the bent of Nature will always reassert itself, a problem all the more intractable because Nature is the point of intersection of all real worlds, if only we could know where it was.

14 Look into the loopholes

CONCLUSION

We knew from the outset that stupid or oafish action and speech prompt reciprocity. People who want to eradicate idiots, or who treat their opponents as idiots, thus make active contributions to the spread of idiocy in the environment. That's why we could only get to grips with idiots as through a mirror, and why in the end this book urges you to reckon you are most likely *more stupid* after having read it than you were before. Because you now know that defending intelligence does not mean thinking yourself clever or knowledgeable; it means asserting, in your innermost self, a pure wish to learn. That is to say, to think of yourself as *a subject who is theoretically wrong*.

Yes, indeed: fools and knaves have taught us that there is no expert at dealing with stupidity and that you have to constantly think up new tricks and devices to get around this strange and chaotic phenomenon. What's more, and forgive me for saying so, as long as you have your nose in this book, you go on being *a subject who is theoretically wrong*. Only when you come up against an idiot or a boor who you identify as a perfectly authentic instance of the phenomenon will you show your valour and your values, and then your 'being right' will cease to be theoretical.

To state the argument in the shortest way possible: we have seen how idiots prompt in us a particular emotional state; that this state marks the end of trust; that this interactional collapse is mutual and destroys all ability to communicate; and as contact is progressively lost, we wish increasingly to restore it by means of authority. Such authority is only clumsily established by the use of insults or vulgar language, by reference to morality or the law, or by other reactions of all kinds that serve one and only one function: to restore the force of the broken link by giving it a different form – an aggressive, violent, dominant and even destructive posture. So as to avoid stumbling into a war on idiots, which would be a war of all against all, we can only alternate between three strategies: negotiating with those who can manage it, changing those who allow it, and leaving those who refuse to change on their own.

In the end, our investigation has brought to the surface a dimension of human life that exists and persists irrespective of stupidity in all its forms: those fragile and yet indestructible ties of interdependence which, for better or worse, make our existences inseparable from each other. Those intangible umbilical cords that tie us together, those mental connections that link our brains, those pangs of joy and anger that pass from one's nerve ends to another's should remind us that individuals arise from their interactions *before* groups and institutions can emerge from people's preferences and activities, and that such entities *only* arise from interactions between individuals.

That's how it is. Despite what you hear from bar-room

loudmouths and village grandmas, solidarity isn't something we've lost and need to restore. Whether we want to or not, whether we know it or not, solidarity – and this is the awkward thing – can't be lost. 'Solidarity' should be used not so much to mean the decision to be generous as to refer to the mode by which interactions work. They can be composed of or be decomposed into infinite variations; they are the informally invented rules of chaos itself.

In that sense, the first foundation of stupidity is probably the universally shared wish to exist as separate beings. That wish is opposed to its complementary desire, which is to belong; and because of this, it seeks to hear only what it asserts, to foresee only what it imagines itself, to see no implementation other than the means it dreams of having or already possesses. There's nothing more obstinate, blind and obscurantist than the desire for separate existence, and because of its legitimate tendency towards the least effort, every human being stumbles again and again into its most idiotic form, and has to dig deep into the very soil of desire to find the means of getting out of it. The madness of desire, which is wanting to possess everything, the absurd pride in joy or sadness, this blindness in knowledge as in ignorance, this contempt for others in happiness as in misfortune, this deafness in dialogue as in silence – we all rise up from these things or else wallow in them every morning, but everyone ends up sinking into them sooner or later. That's also why it is agreeable to *play the fool*, as it is a way of taking time out from the permanent struggle between separation and connectedness, between the striving for autonomy and the striving towards belonging.

What I think I have realised in writing this essay on interactional ethics as if it were a letter to the faithful is how hard we all find it to keep a balance between imposing norms by force (which aggravates the destruction of interactions between people) and relativistic renunciation (which does the same thing, in an opposite way). That's why contempt for idiots, which arises at both extremes, is insufficient on its own. On closer inspection, all pathologies of interaction – idiots being a symptom of such pathologies – teach us to be attentive to the kinds of interdependence that they reveal. So I'm not yet done with interactional ethics, far from it. In it, I see enlightening ways of describing other problems we face today.

If you want neither to scale back the anger that idiots of all varieties arouse in you nor to let it fade away, then you will have to sort yourself out so as to make room – yes, just make a space – for your opponents, so that they stop getting on your nerves and can themselves find in the balance of forces a more or less dignified way out. But I warned you about this before: they won't let you do it. While you try to assert yourself as a peace-making force, they'll go on asserting themselves as forces of war. In daily life, you will not always be able to avoid instances of diplomacy in which you welcome and integrate the sufferings of boors and idiots, or instances of open conflict, where you reject their suffering and just let them rant and rave. In all cases, idiots will teach you more than you will teach them, because you are the one who wishes to learn. And may I remind you that in the interim the cosmic equilibrium will remain entirely indifferent to peace as to war.

Philosophers have tried to see some kind of ultimate serenity or wisdom in the indifference of the universe. But as I announced in the opening pages of this book, to reach a state of wisdom that could vaporise all idiots with a single stare you would have to be either God herself, or already dead – and also indifferent as to which of those two states you enjoy. In *this* sub-lunar world, no conflict ever ends without trace, without someone feeling beaten, humiliated or wronged. As a result, stupidity will always rise from its ashes with the same alacrity as it celebrates its victories. Idiots will therefore always laugh at your *so-called* virtue, and their suffering will always stand against your *so-called* striving for peace. So instead of pretending to find a third way, peace has no alternative but to take the energy of war on board, and to accept the necessity of conflicts as a *game*. That's right. That is the reality and the morality of History on the individual as well as the collective plane: it's a vast game of separations and reunions that is tragic and comical in equal measure. If instead of making your anguish the *stake*, you manage to assuage it by *playing the game*, then for a few minutes before you finally exit this mortal stage you will have a seat at the table where gods and philosophers laugh out loud and throw insults at each other.

Acknowledgements

I would like to thank most especially Luiz Camillo Osorio, Director of the Department of Philosophy at the Pontifícia Universidade Católica in Rio de Janeiro, Jimena Solé of the Universidad de Buenos Aires and Helena Urfer at the Université de Montréal (UdM) for having provided the conditions without which this investigation of interactional ethics could not have been conducted.

My thanks also go to Annelore Parot, Aurélien Robert, Diane Lançon, Maxime Catroux, Pauline Hartmann and Ronan de Calan for having shared with me their sufferings and their insights. And, of course, to Camila, *que explora com tanto carinho e tanta coragem as brechas do meu mundo.*

Bibliography

Some readers will have recognised the sources of my ideas, and those who didn't might find it useful to consult the following philosophical works. As I didn't look back at them while writing this book, I didn't think it appropriate to acknowledge them in footnotes.

Jürgen Habermas, *Justification and Application: Remarks on Discourse Ethics*, transl. Ciaran Cronin. Cambridge, MA: MIT Press, 1993.

Axel Honneth, *The Struggle for Recognition: The Moral Grammar of Social Conflicts* (1949), transl. Joel Anderson. Cambridge, MA: Polity Press, 1995.

Immanuel Kant, *The Metaphysics of Morals* (1785), transl. Mary Gregor. Cambridge, UK: Cambridge University Press, 1991.

Étienne de La Boétie, *The Politics of Obedience: The Discourse of Voluntary Servitude* (1576), transl. Harry Kurz. New York: Free Life Editions, 1975.

Friedrich Nietzsche, *On the Genealogy of Morals* (1887), transl. Michael Scarpitti. London: Penguin, 2013.

Leopold von Sacher-Masoch, *Venus in Furs* (1870), transl. Joachim Neugroschel. New York: Penguin, 2000.

Donatien de Sade, *Justine, Philosophy in the Bedroom, and Other Writings* (1791), transl. Richard Seaver and Austryn Wainhouse. New York: Grove, 1966.

Peter Sloterdijk, *Not Saved: Essays after Heidegger*, transl. I. A. Moore and C. Turner. Cambridge, MA: Polity Press, 2016.

Max Stirner, *The Ego and Its Own* (1845), transl. Steven Byington, ed. David Leopold. Cambridge, UK: Cambridge University Press, 1995.